AF477428

Donald Baechler

EARLY WORK 1980 TO 1984

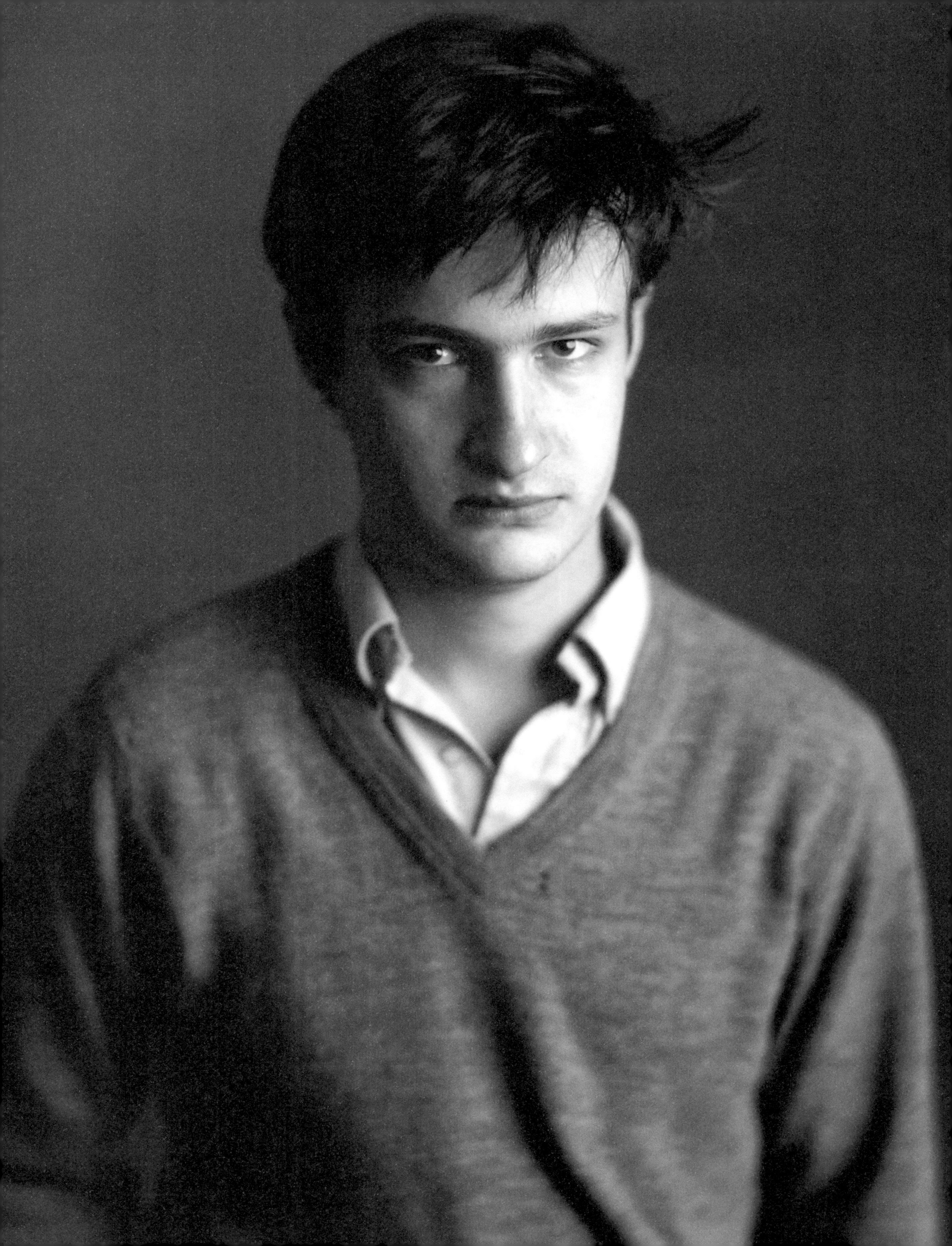

Donald Baechler

EARLY WORK 1980 TO 1984

ESSAY BY DAVID RIMANELLI

CHEIM & READ NEW YORK

You Were Not Elected President, Yet Won the Race

David Rimanelli

Donald Baechler's iconography is drawn from a kind of
mythic world that is customarily described as childlike. The
sense of incompleteness, the apparent simplicity of his
forms has often led writers in this direction, but here, as
elsewhere, childhood becomes a placeholder for encounters
where conventional uses of language and representation
fail. There are parallels: Baechler's frequent use of
white grounds may be seen in accord with the analyst's
description of the "the terrible pallor" of the child watching
a sibling nursing at the breast—a bloodless paralysis, the
overwhelming totality of infantile sexuality, the immersion
in helpless rage and fear—this is childhood, not as
"dysfunctional," but as both common and unspeakable,
which finds an echo in Baechler's layered whiteness.

Baechler's inventiveness bears witness to a marriage of
awkwardness and grace, layering, erasure, desperation—the
unmaking and remaking of a language of sublimation and
subversion. Titles function as disclaimers throughout the
project, and the works show a cosmopolitan twist to subject
matter that travels from suburban tract houses to resorts in

Caracas. *Inflatable Sex Toy*, 1980, reminiscent of Warhol's portraits of Mick Jagger, conveys a knowingly submerged sexuality in its liquid half-vacant face surrounded by a blue halo. Works from the *Monotone Drawing* series, 1981, position what appears to be an armless Pre-Columbian statue against electric coffee pots and business suits—the icons from an '80s Talking Heads LP. Elsewhere, Iberian statuary appears against a backdrop of red-and-white stripes, with an apparent randomness that suggests Jasper Johns' interest in chance as well as the American flag. This history of chance is one offering both invention and the possibility of an alibi. It could have happened differently, it could have been someone else. As Baechler says, "One reason I build my surfaces up is because I don't really want to know what the line is going to do. I want this built-in fracture; when I drag the brush along the canvas I don't want it to be a smooth, easy voyage—I want some problems along the way."[1] These problems, and the overcoming of them, become the points of tension and discovery in the paintings.

There is a lot of effort in all of this—this appearance of "simplicity." Baechler collects and archives thousands of images but uses only a few; he scrapes, erases, and paints "fists of fury"—the title of a work from 1983. I am reminded of John Ashbery's language of struggle:

What had you been thinking about
the face studiously bloodied
heaven blotted region
I go on loving you like water but
There is a terrible breath in the way of all of this
You were not elected president, yet won the race
        —Ashbery, "The Tennis Court Oath"[2]

This indexing of a different kind of winning, of work that brings blood to the face, and in later verses, stammering and worry, courses throughout these early works of Baechler. There is a kinship here with his labored reinvention of painterly language—painterly *syntax*. The work appears self-chosen, the victory ambiguous. Harold Bloom, although a champion of Ashbery's work, disparaged the poems in *The Tennis Court Oath*, calling them artificial, a result of "his association with the 'New York School' of Kenneth Koch, Frank O'Hara and other comedians of the spirit."[3] This volume, written while Ashbery was living, for the first time, outside the U.S. distances itself from the tradition of American poets such as Whitman and Emerson, and finds an affinity with the self-reflexivity, surrealism, and existentialist gestures of Modernist painting. The writer's position is established as uncertain, unfinished; the standard accolades are not in evidence, yet a different measure of success is achieved.

It is possible, even easy, to find essays on Ashbery's poem "They Dream Only of America" that discuss children and murderers in an entirely literal way, never grasping the gay narrative that unfolds within and between the lines:

They dream only of America
To be lost among the thirteen million pillars of grass:
"This honey is delicious
Though it burns the throat."

More than the references to Whitman's grass, or the honey that burns the throat, it is Ashbery's reordering of language as difference that conveys the poem's deliriously secretive sexual adventures.

And hiding from darkness in barns
They can be grownups now
And the murderer's ash tray is more easily—
The lake a lilac cube.
                    —Ashbery, "They Dream Only of America"[4]

This same conflation of innocence and exoticism haunts Baechler's paintings. In the paintings of *Oum Kalsoum*, 1981, this renowned, and virtually deified, Egyptian singer is portrayed, using the barest of painterly means, and the

inevitable surrealism of photographs deprived of their
captions, as a glamorous relic of Sixties style, her dark
glasses and headscarf congeal into a mask and costume
hinting of all that will not be shown. Barely a fragment,
her image is compelling because it refuses exposure, the
reduction to that which is recognized and named. The
fragment cannot be known, but it can be owned, and here,
possession takes precedence over knowledge.

For the most part, in these early works, the images are
very pale, washed-out, fading. The contrast between these
and his later paintings—those of the characteristic built-up
and then erased surfaces—is striking. Some of the works
from this "early period" do however point towards that
direction, for instance *Study for "Sins of Omission,"* 1983.
Although these works tend to come toward the end of Early,
i.e., 1983–84, there appears to be a break, a sudden shift
from the wan, transitory fragility of the early Early and the
later Early. Those paintings with the built-up and "defaced"
surfaces have a kind of conjured antiquity; there's an
intense archaeological quality. But this "break" is perhaps
deceptive on one crucial level: both the shadowy, ghostlike
works and those of the encrusted, dense painterly facture
concern history, or rather historicity.

Baechler is a compulsive collector of images, images that appear as fragments. Most of these works seem to be on the verge of disappearance, captured for an instant, like a freeze frame or a screen shot. Walter Benjamin writes in "Theses on the Philosophy of History" that "The true picture of the past flits by. The past can be seized only as an image which flashes up at the instant when it can be recognized and is never seen again... For every image of the past that is not recognized by the present as one of its own concerns threatens to disappear irretrievably."[5] Baechler's early works presage his subsequent development as an artist. The image is seized, the past (re)-captured. Who is Oum Kalsoum?

[1]*BOMB*, Summer 2000.
[2]John Ashbery, "The Tennis Court Oath" from *The Tennis Court Oath: A Book of Poems*, Wesleyan University Press, Hanover, New Hampshire, 1962.
[3]*John Ashbery (Bloom's Modern Critical Views)*, Chelsea House, New York, 1985.
[4] John Ashbery, "They Dream Only of America" from *The Tennis Court Oath: A Book of Poems*, Wesleyan University Press, Hanover, New Hampshire, 1962.
[5]Walter Benjamin, *Illuminations: Essays and Reflections*, edited by Hannah Arendt, Schocken Books, New York, 1969.

Three Figures (Wall Street Week) 1980 graphite, spray enamel and oil-based enamel on paper 42 x 42 in 106.7 x 106.7 cm

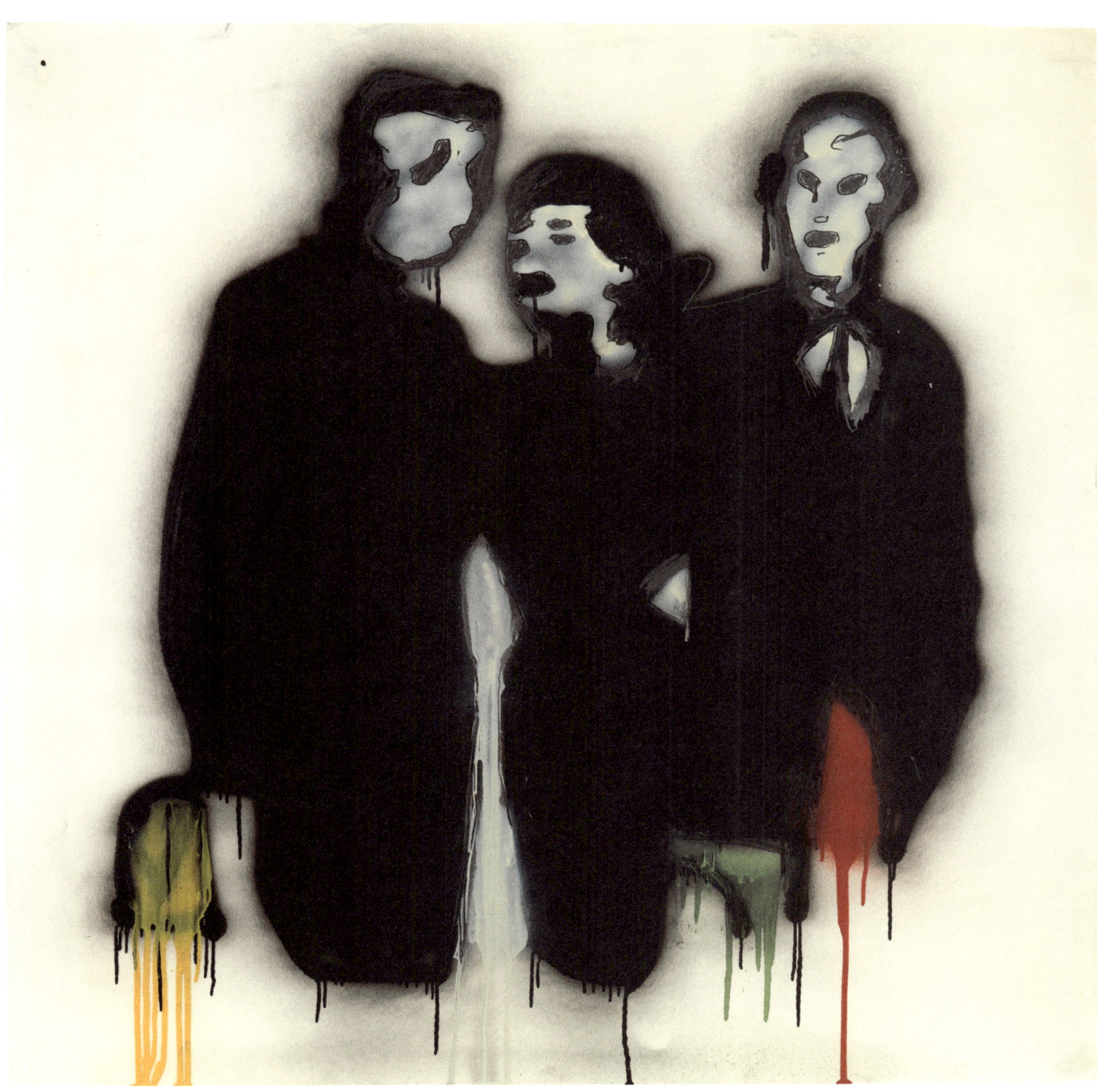

House 1980 graphite, spray enamel and oil-based enamel on paper 42 x 42 in 106.7 x 106.7 cm

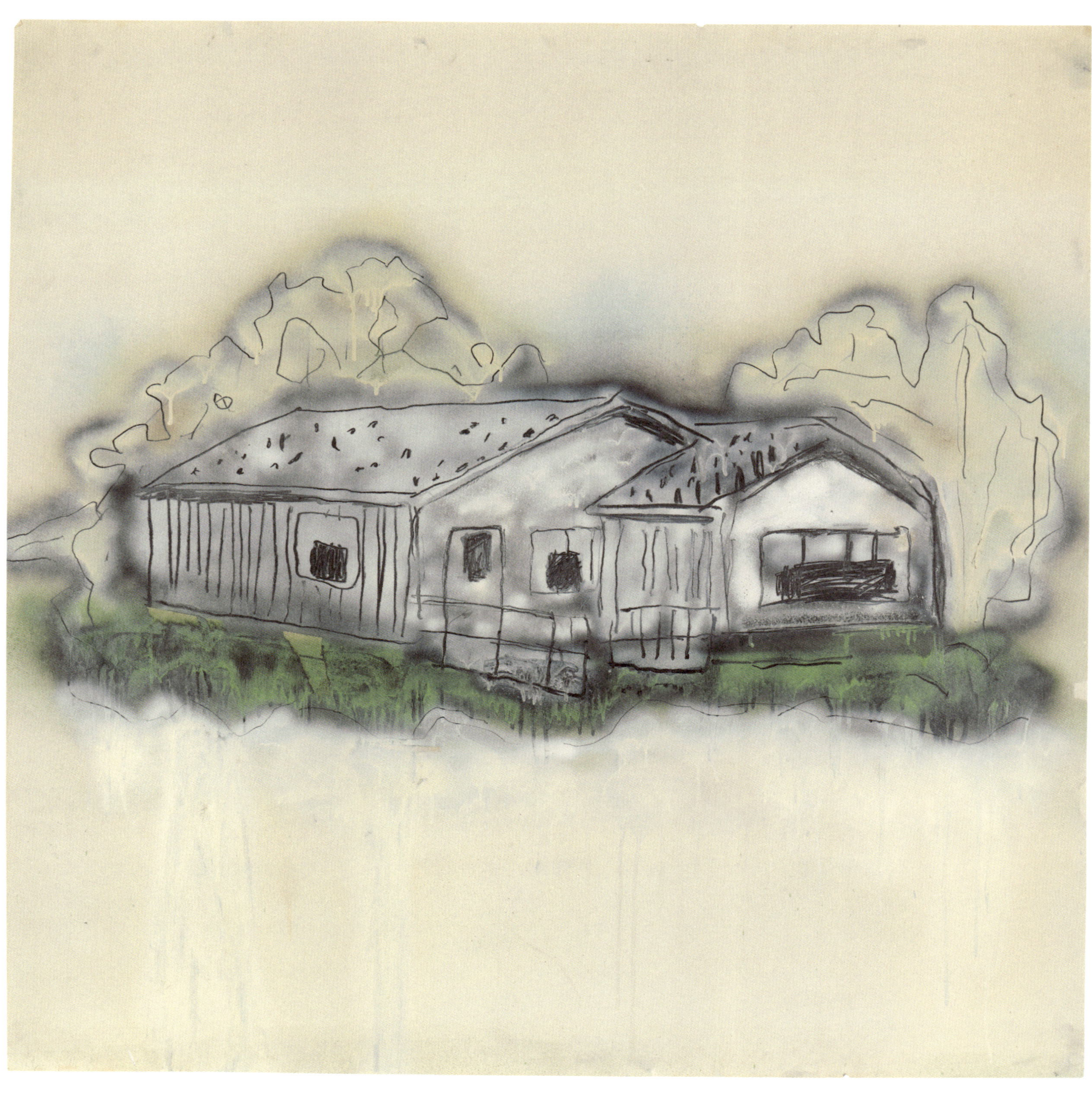

Inflatable Sex Toy 1980 graphite, spray enamel and oil-based enamel on paper 42 x 42 in 106.7 x 106.7 cm

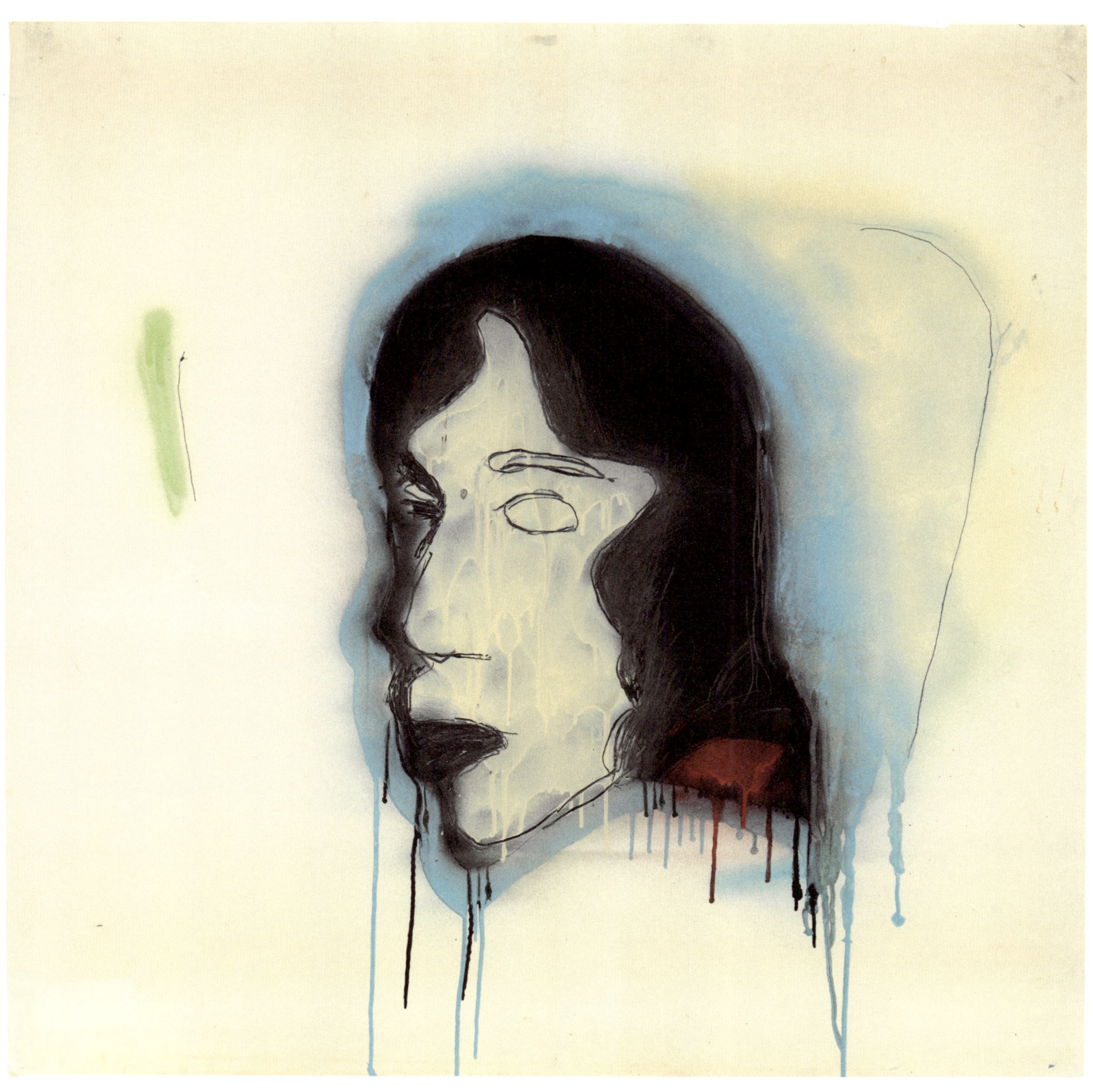

Open City 1980 graphite, spray enamel and oil-based enamel on paper 25 x 38 in 63.5 x 96.5 cm

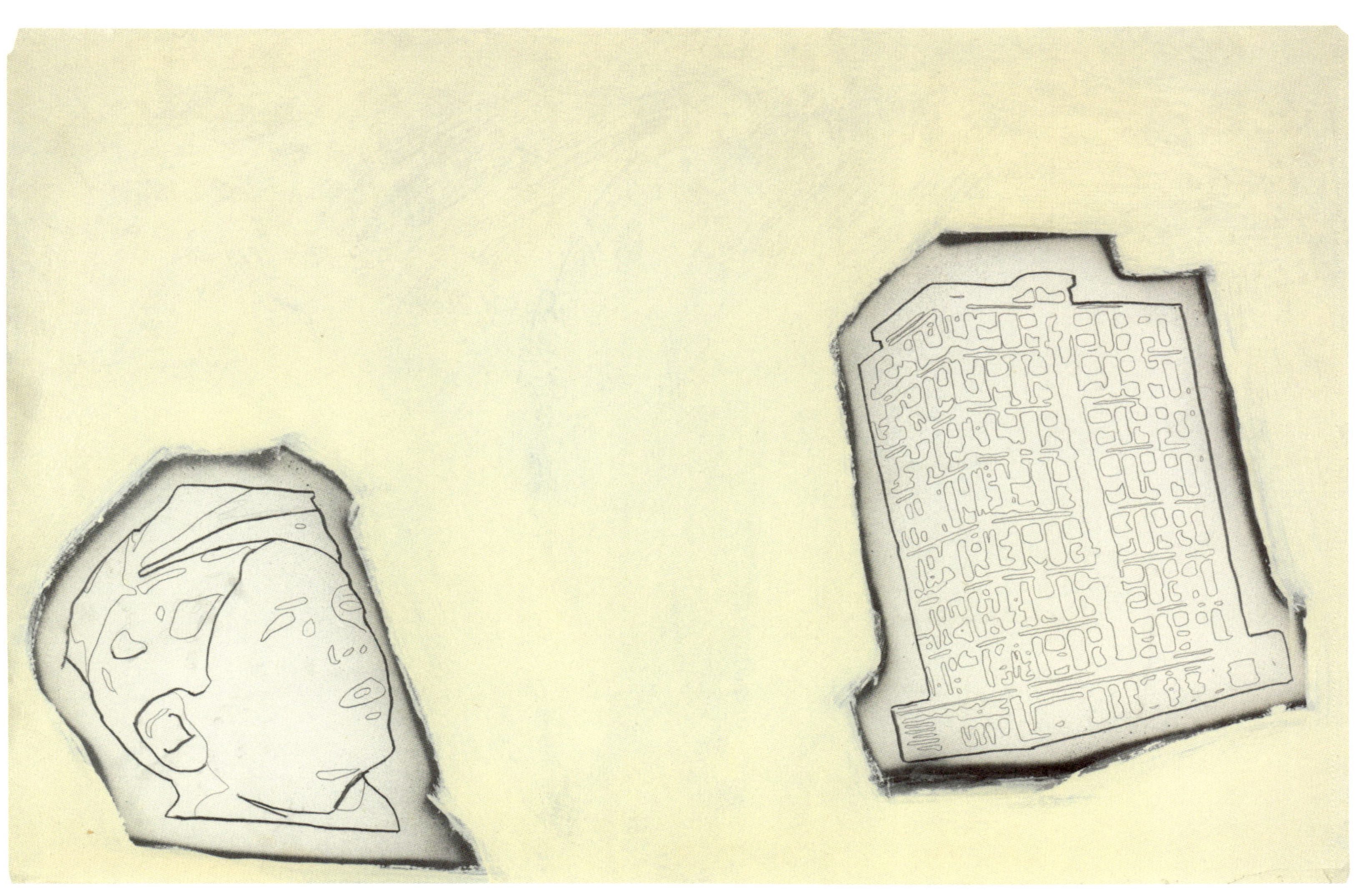

Resort Group 1980 graphite, spray enamel and oil-based enamel on paper 30 x 22 in 76.2 x 55.9 cm

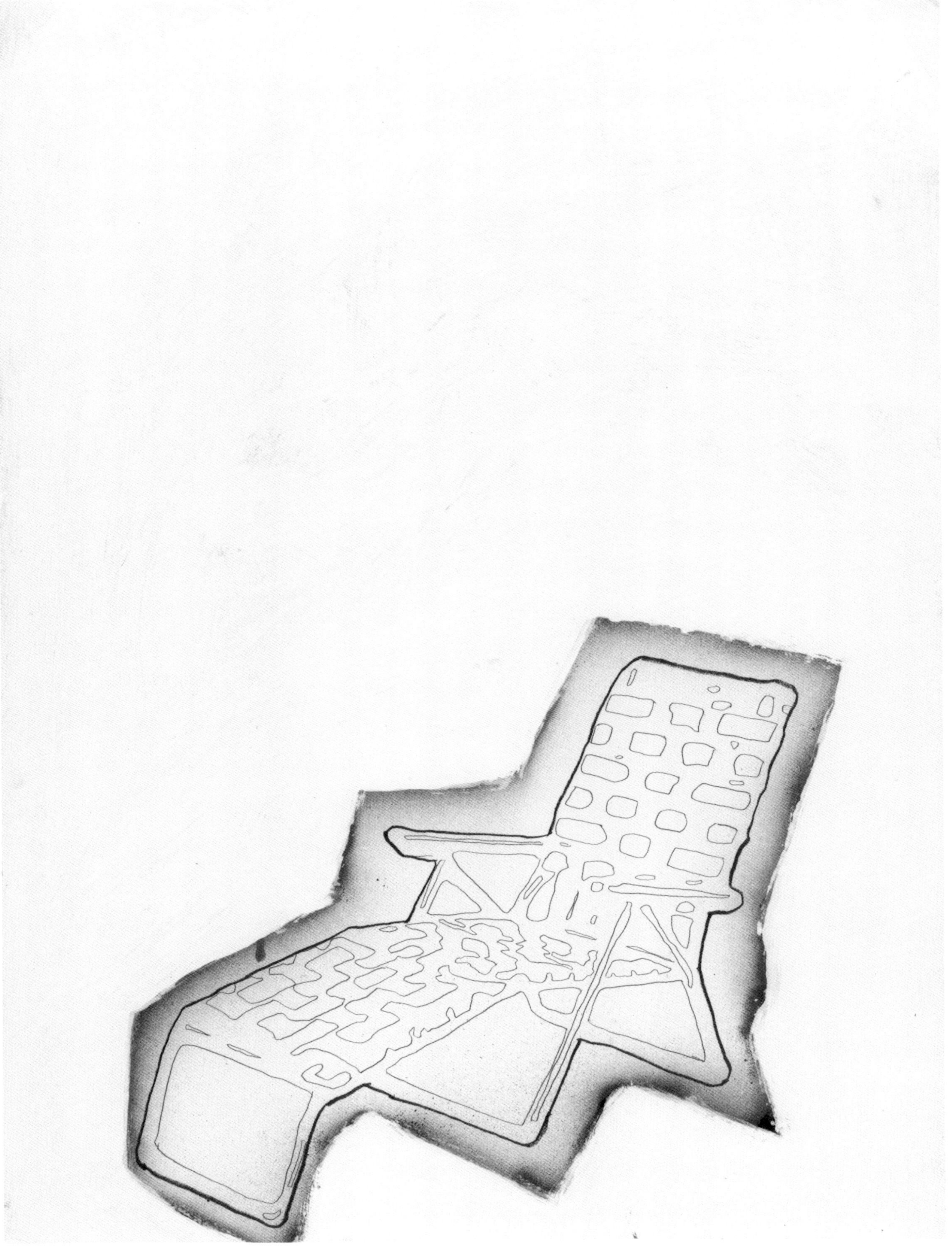

Window 1980 graphite on paper 20 x 20 in 50.8 x 50.8 cm

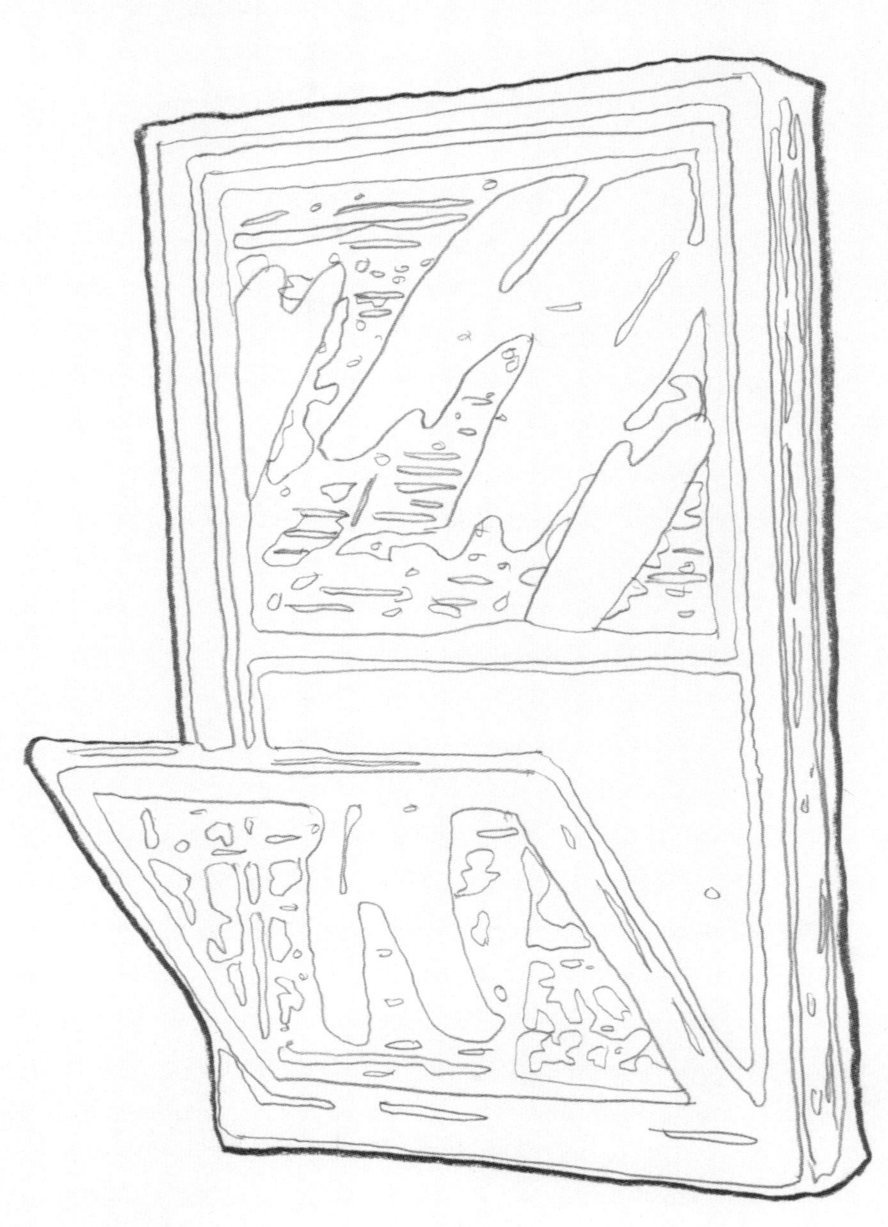

Windows 1980 graphite on paper 20 x 20 in 50.8 x 50.8 cm

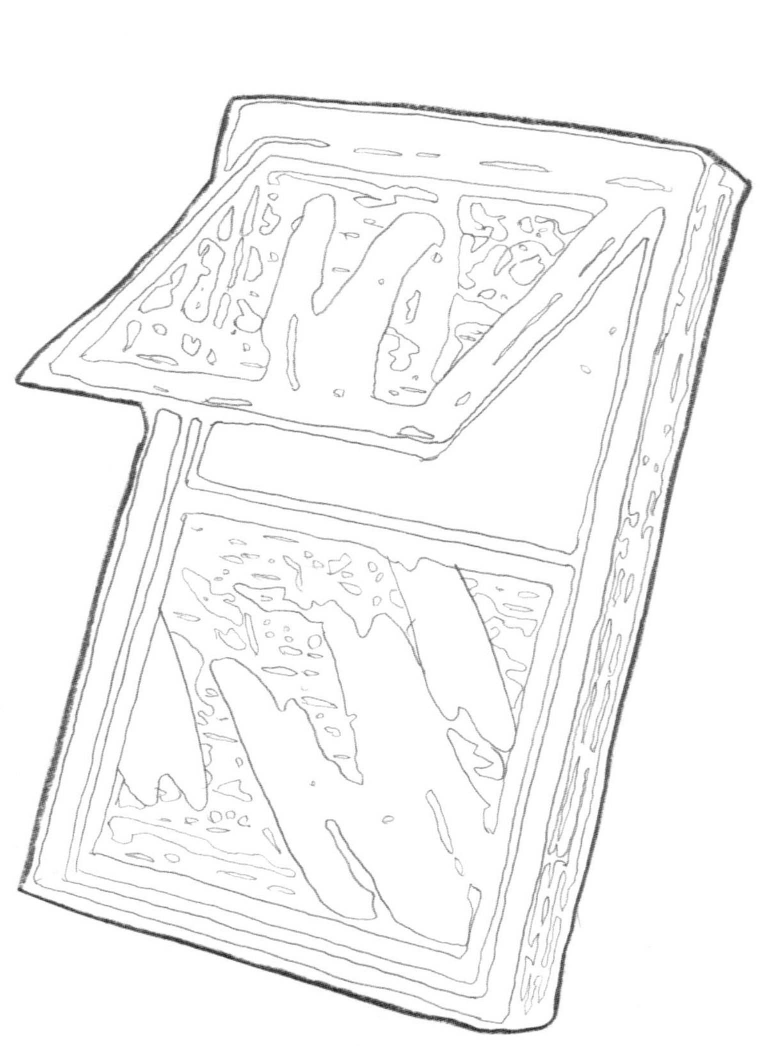
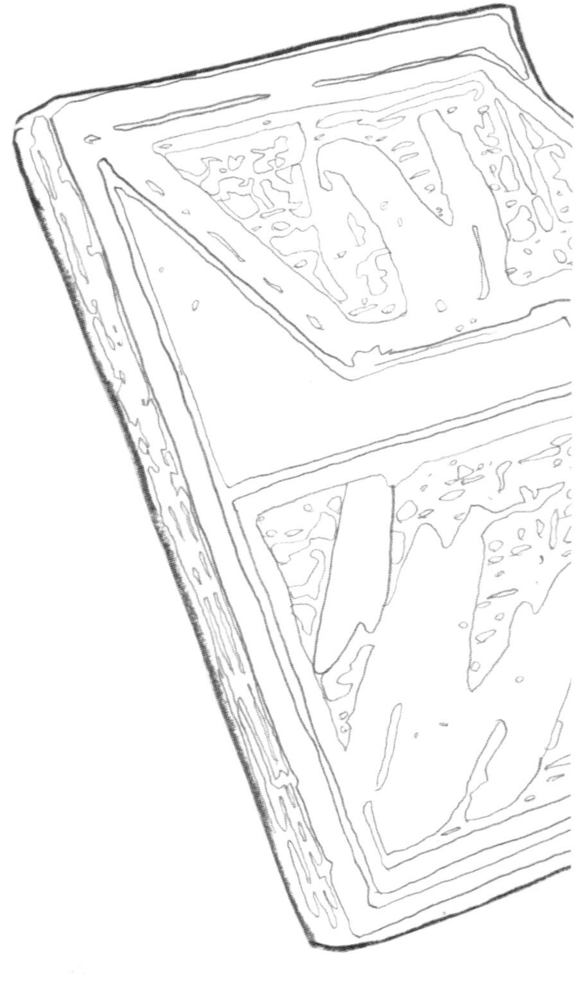

Hotel In Caracas (Resort Group) 1980 graphite, spray enamel and oil-based enamel on paper 42 x 42 in 106.7 x 106.7 cm

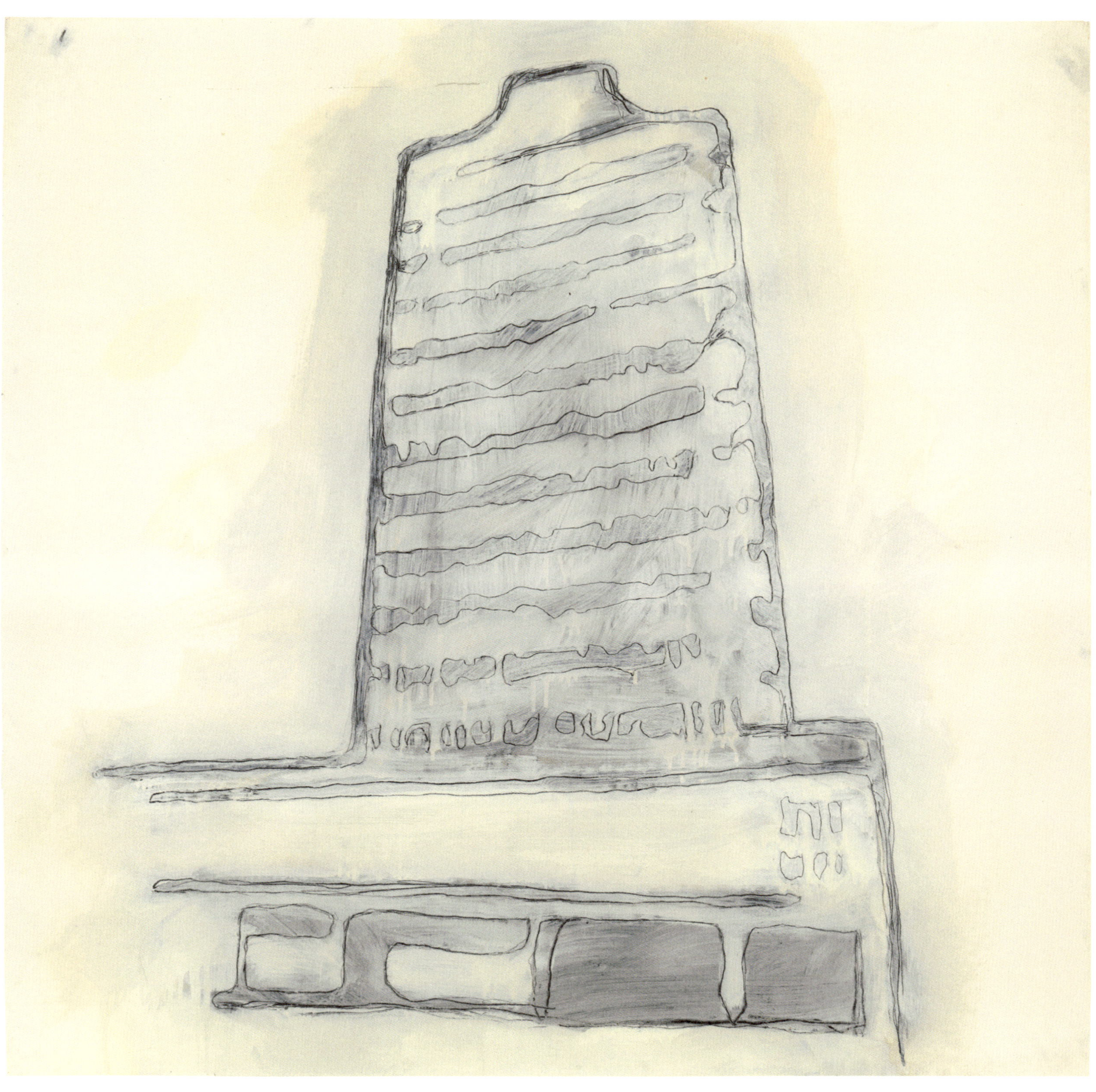

Hand With Box 1980 graphite, spray enamel and oil-based enamel on paper 42 x 42 in 106.7 x 106.7 cm

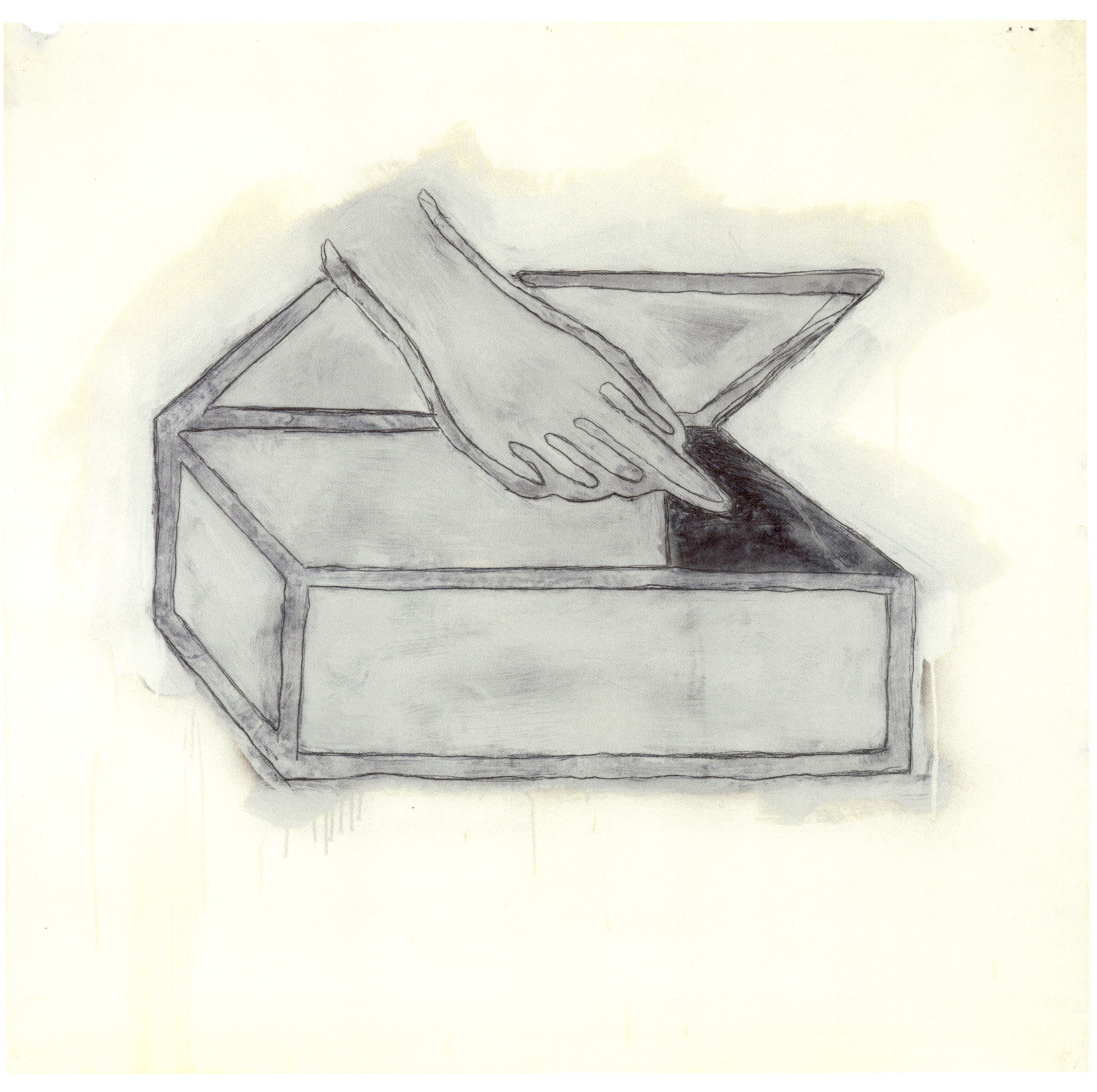

Sign 1981 graphite and oil-based enamel on paper 35 x 46 in 88.9 x 116.8 cm

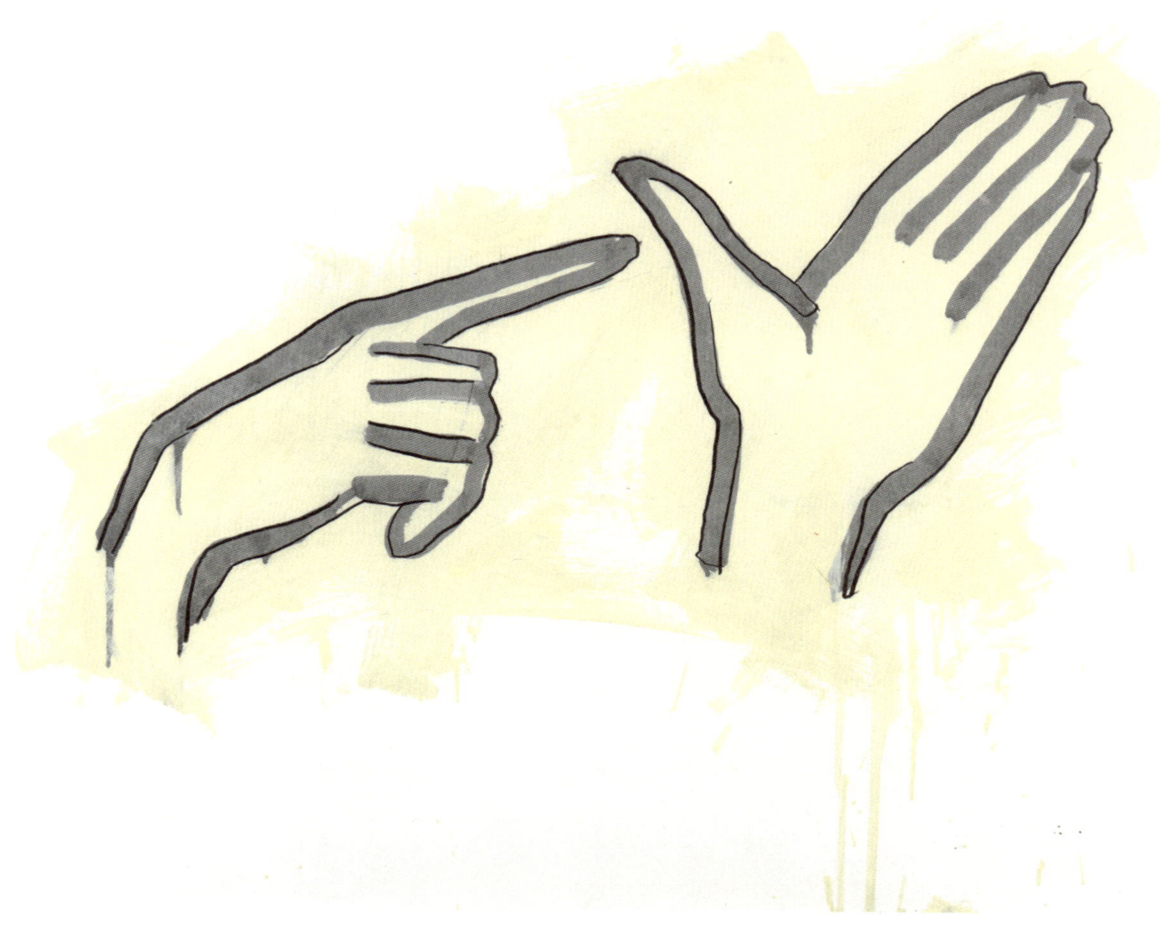

Monotone Drawing 1981 graphite and oil-based enamel on paper 35 x 46 in 88.9 x 116.8 cm

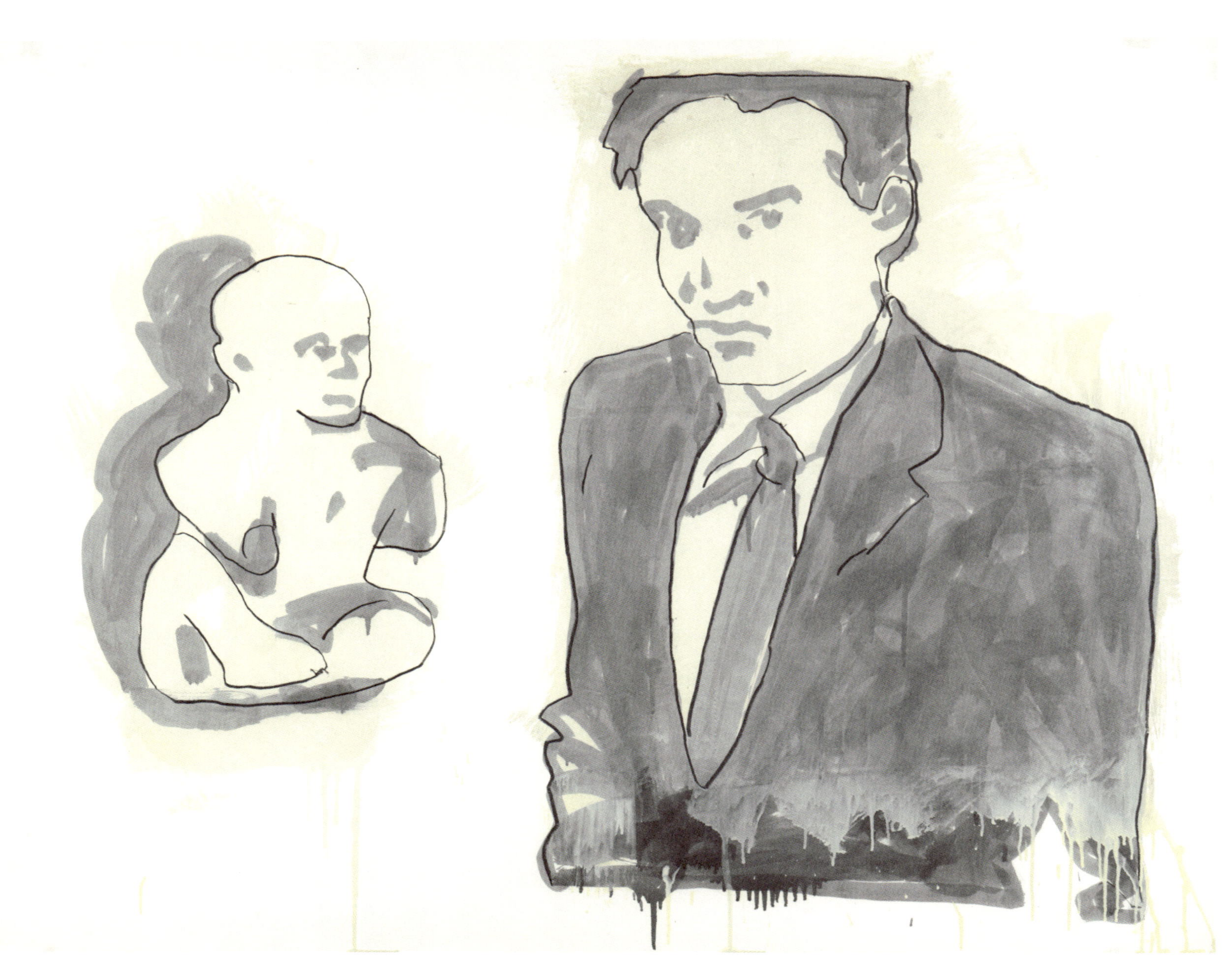

Monotone Drawing 1981 graphite and oil-based enamel on paper 35 x 46 in 88.9 x 116.8 cm

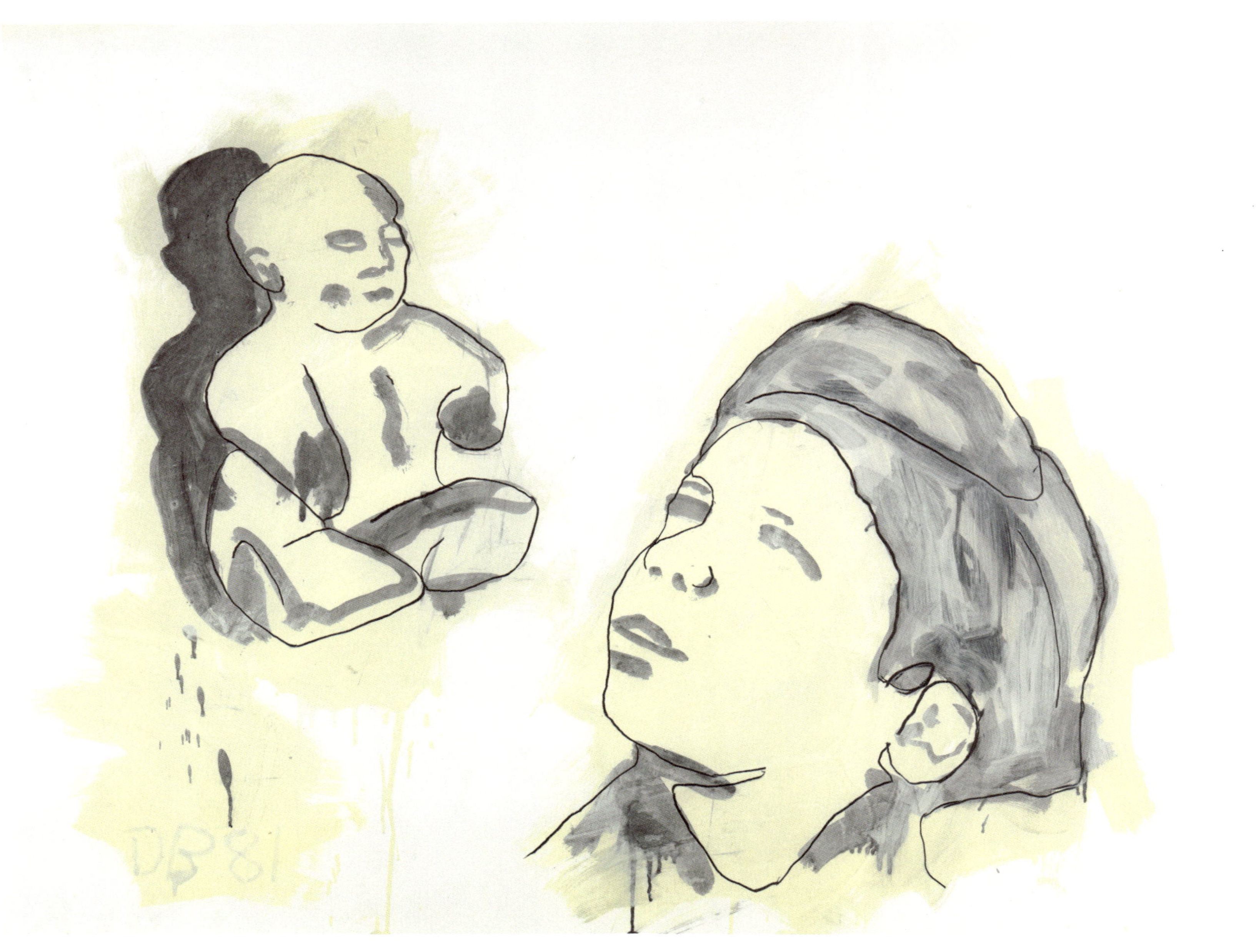
DB 81

Monotone Drawing With Mandolin Player 1981 graphite and oil-based enamel on paper 35 x 46 in 88.9 x 116.8 cm

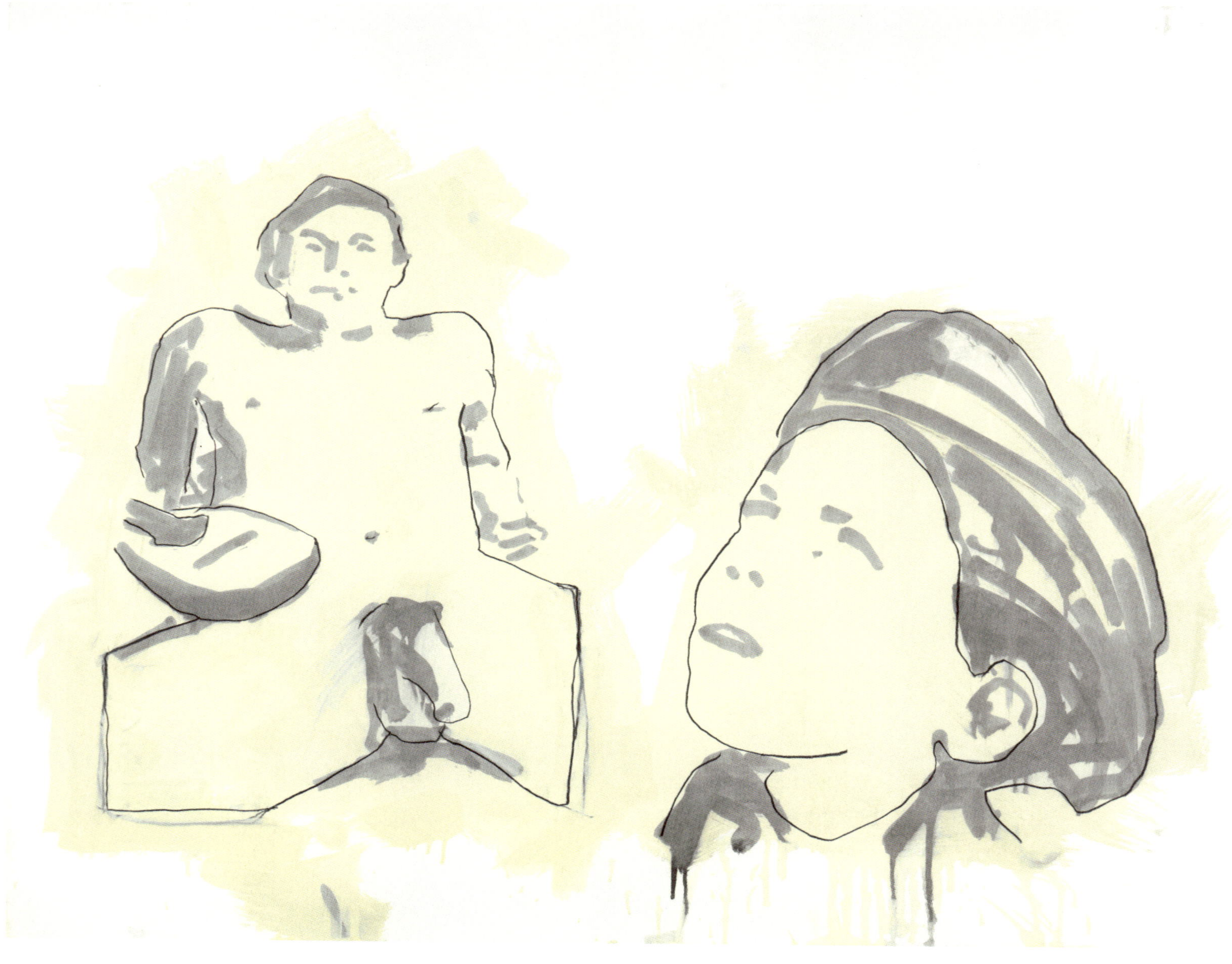

Monotone Drawing 1981 graphite and oil-based enamel on paper 35 x 46 in 88.9 x 116.8 cm

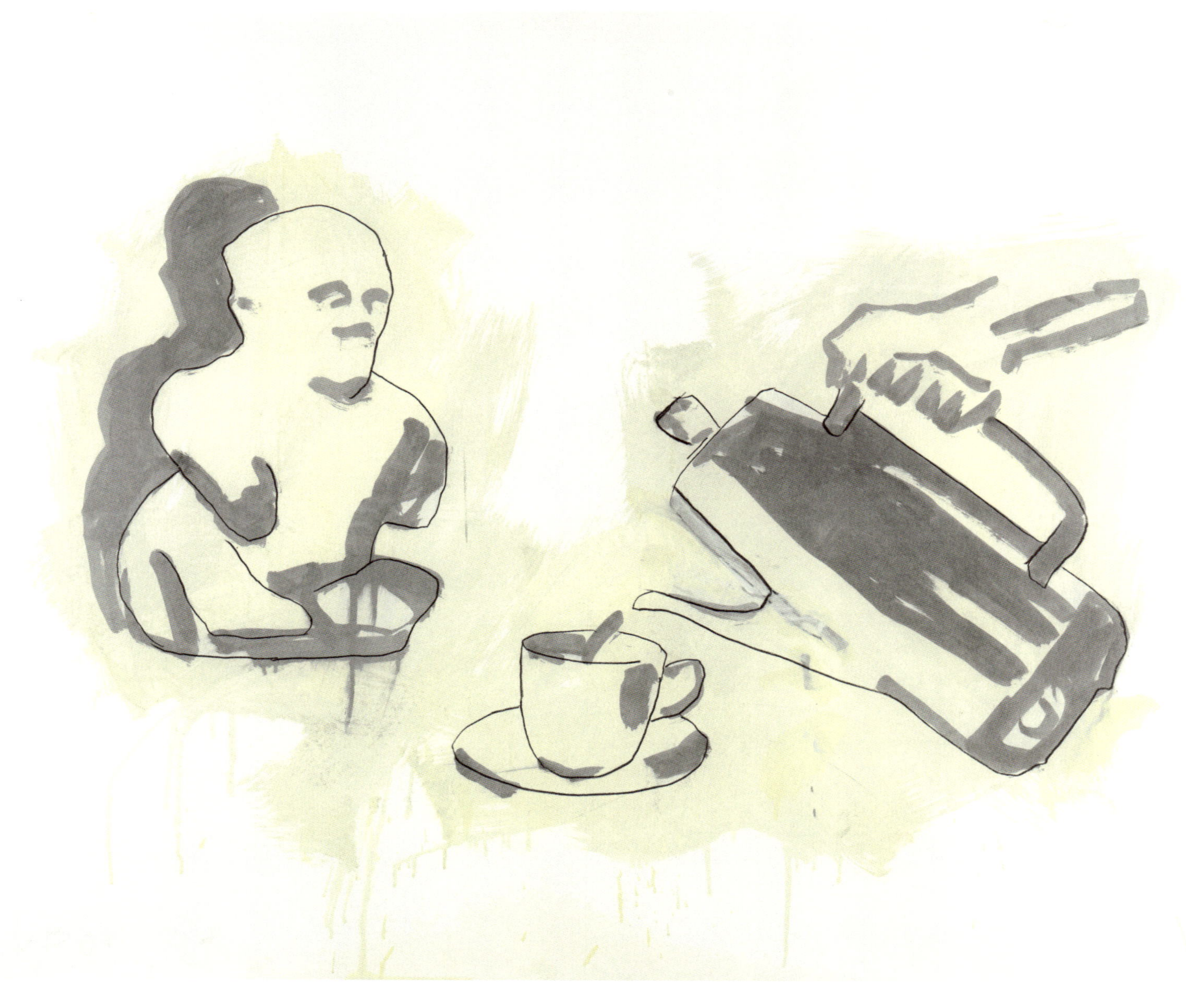

Monotone Drawing 1981 graphite and oil-based enamel on paper 46 x 35 in 116.8 x 88.9 cm

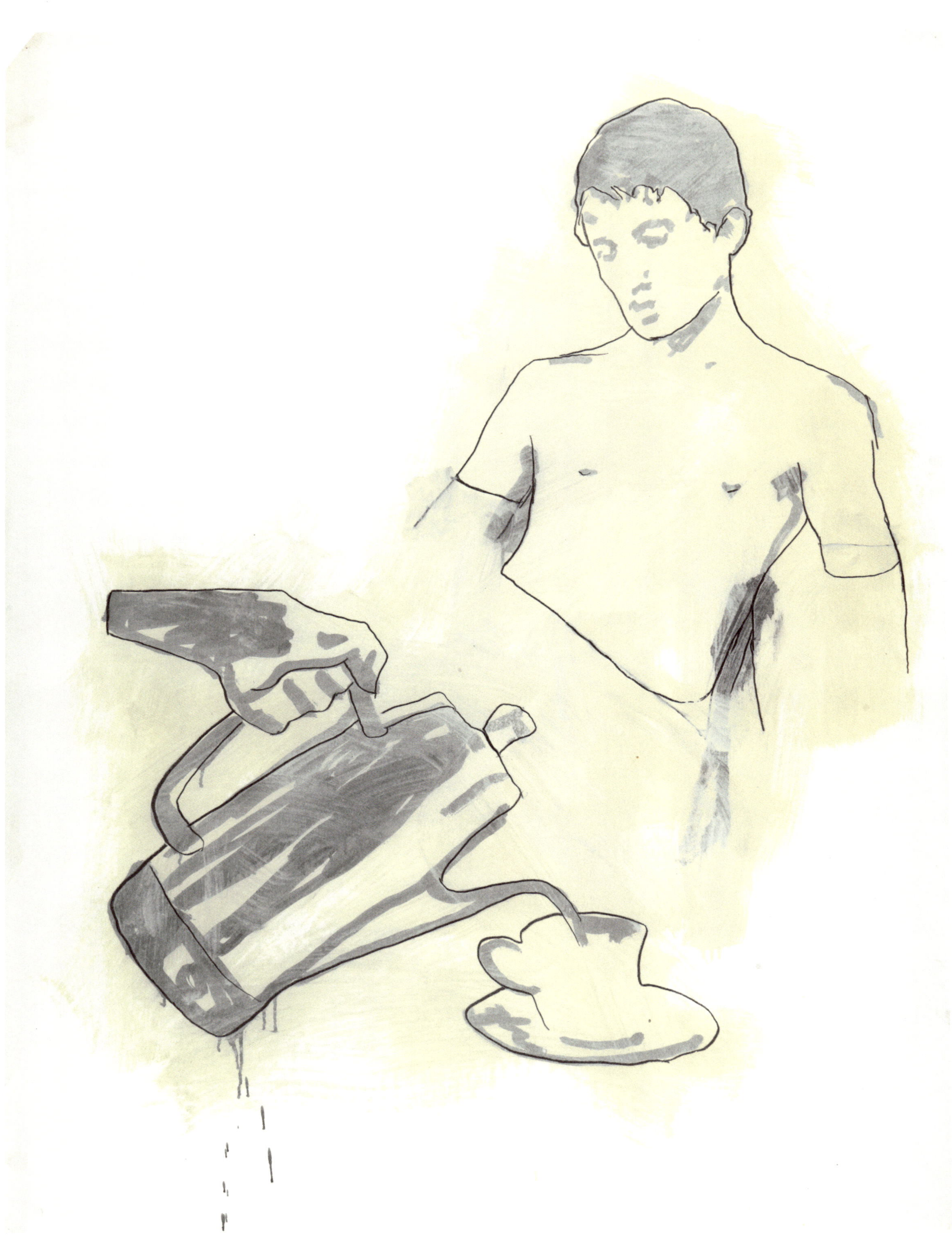

Monotone Drawing With Airplane 1981 graphite and oil-based enamel on paper 35 x 46 in 88.9 x 116.8 cm

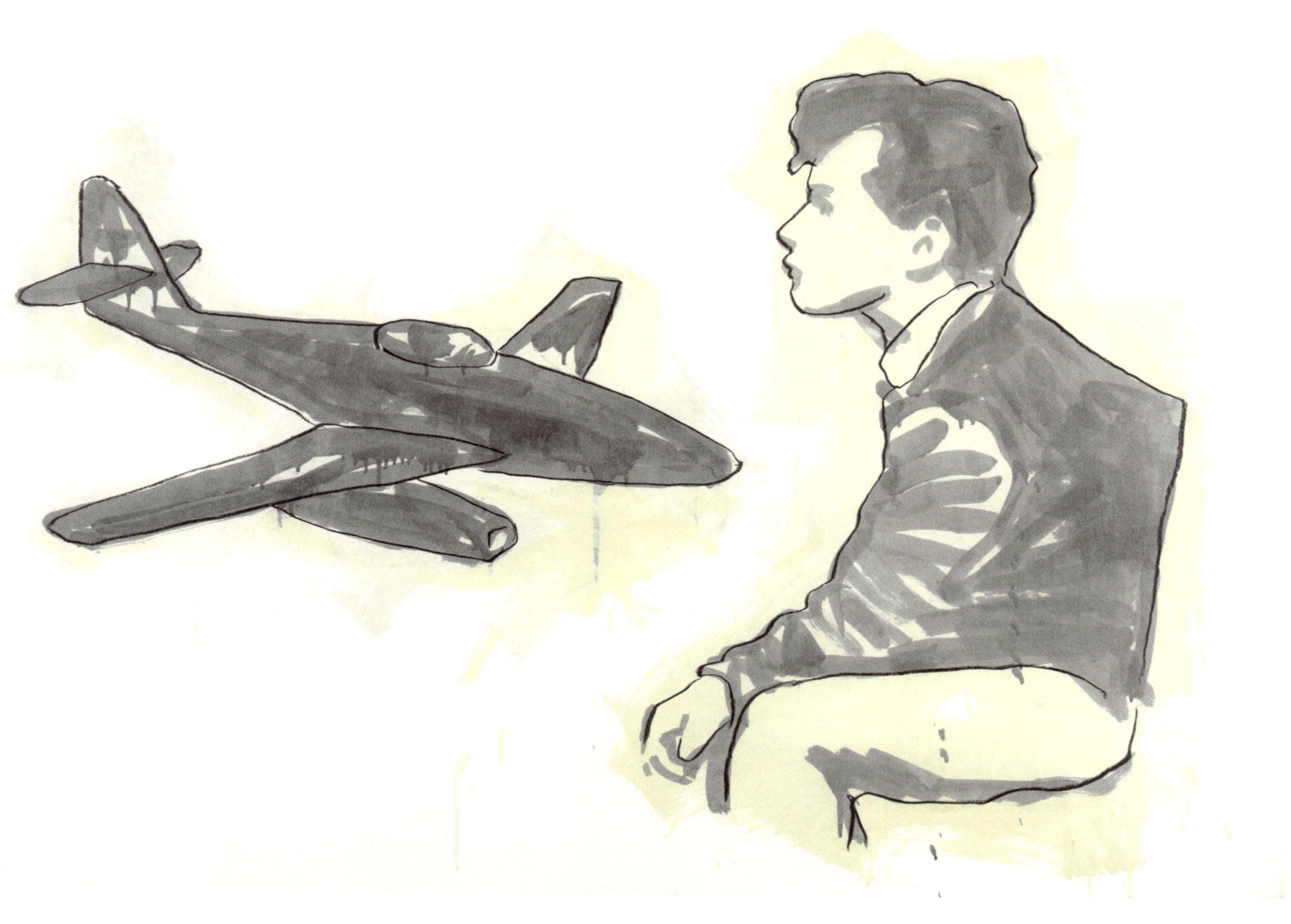

Monotone Drawing 1981 graphite and oil-based enamel on paper 35 x 46 in 88.9 x 116.8 cm

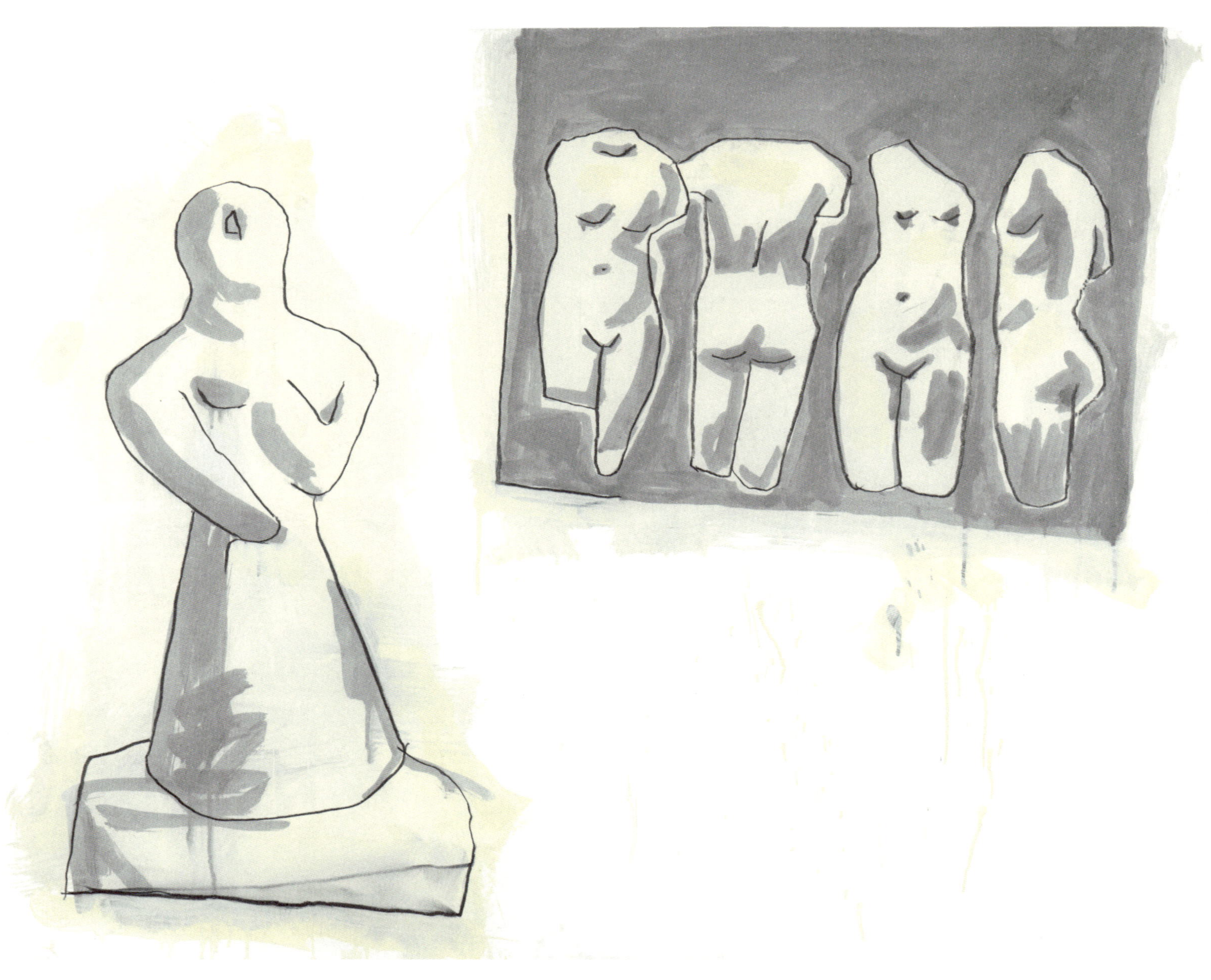

Vocabulary Lesson 1981 graphite and oil-based enamel on paper 35 x 46 in 88.9 x 116.8 cm

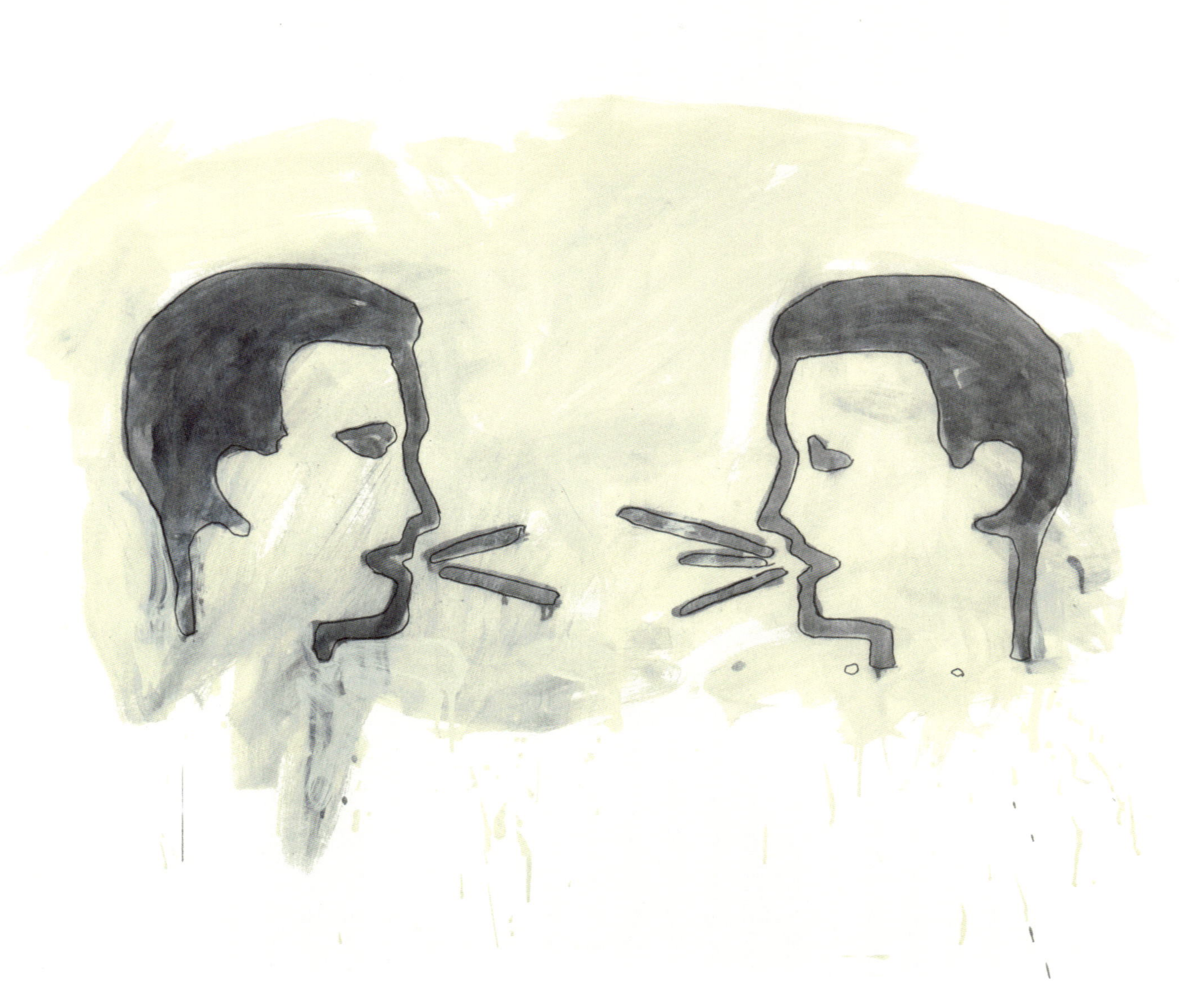

Sphinx 1981 graphite and oil-based enamel on paper 46 x 35 in 116.8 x 88.9 cm

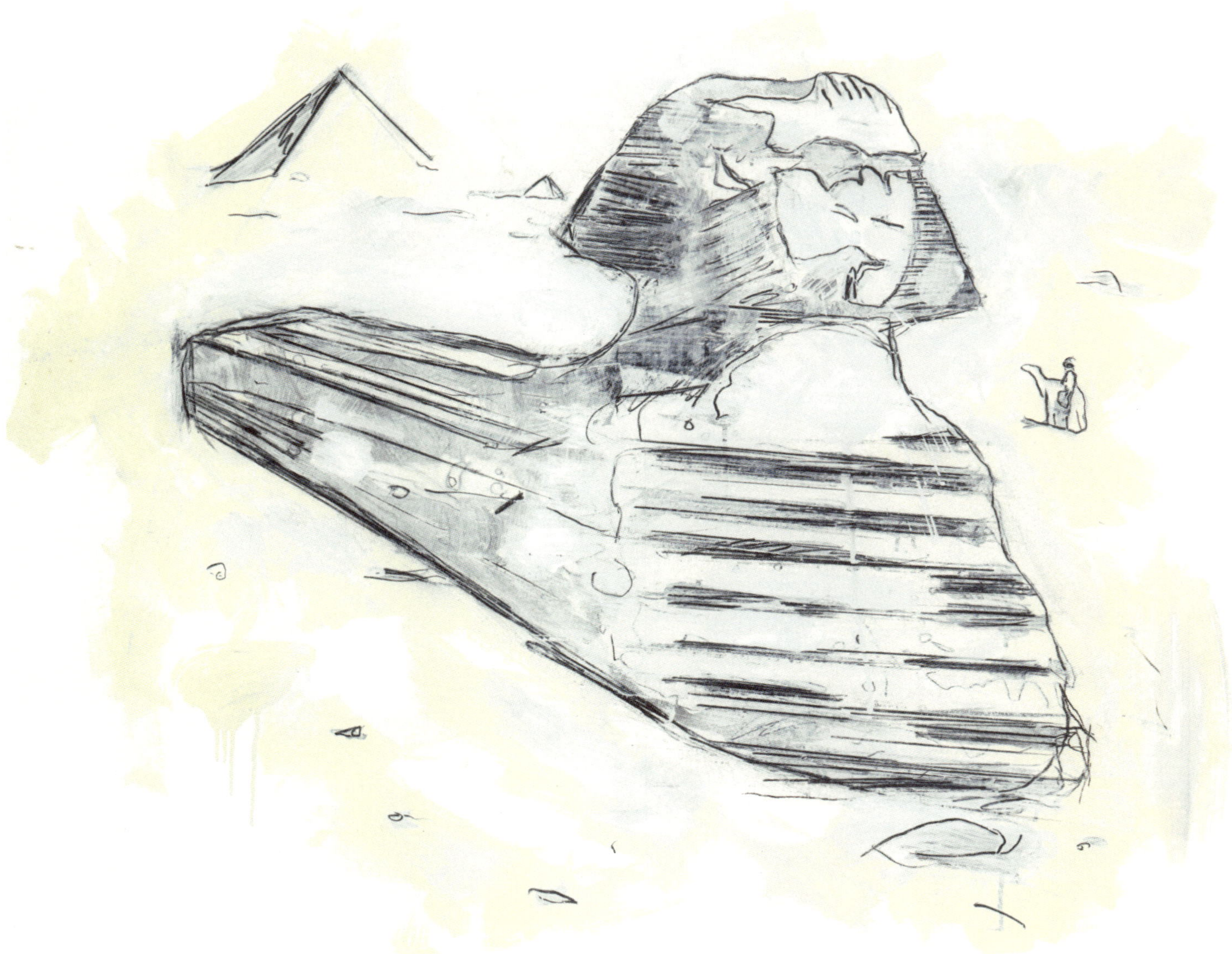

Suburban House Drawing 1981 graphite and oil-based enamel on paper 35 x 46 in 88.9 x 116.8 cm

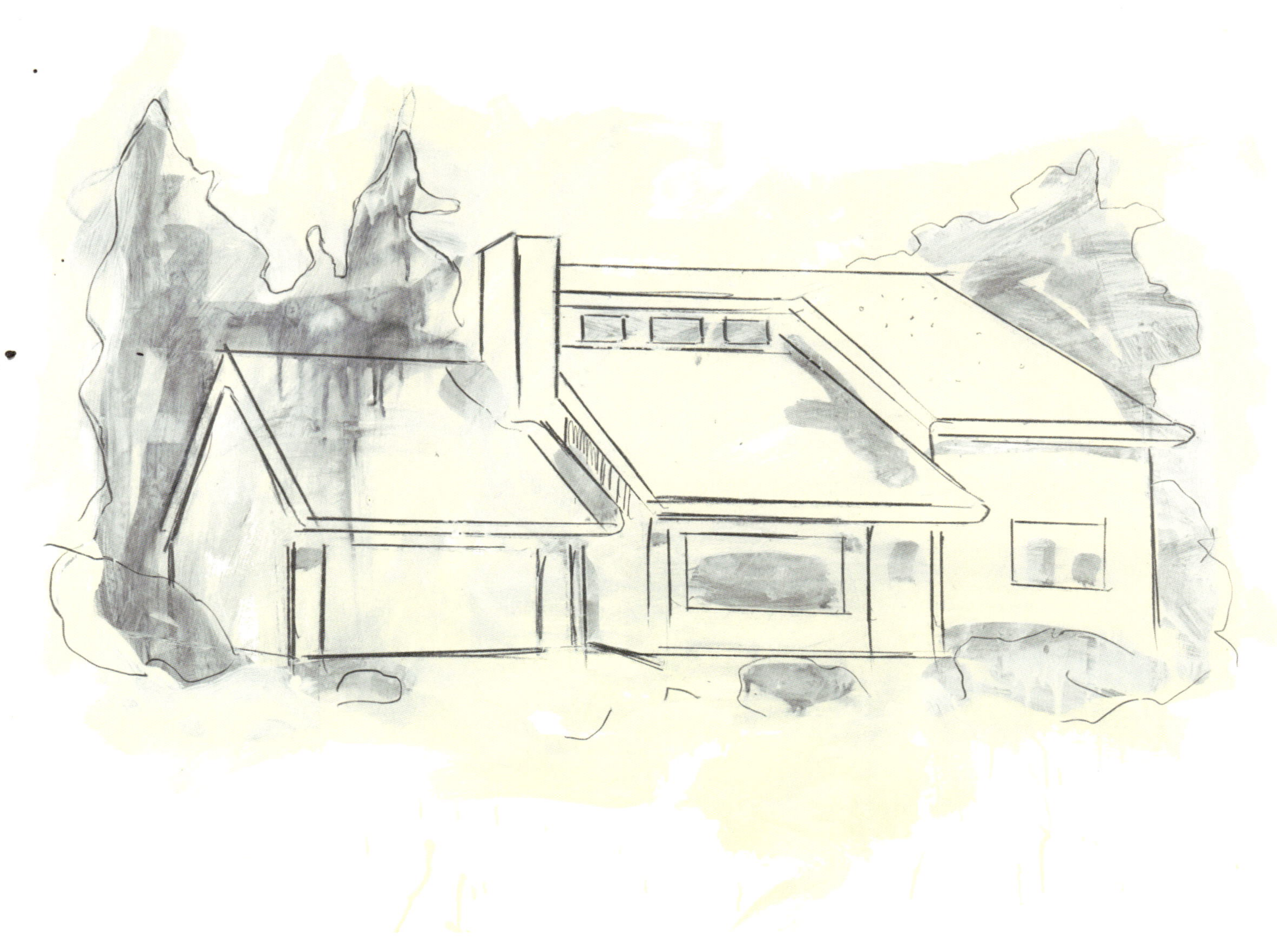

Sink 1981 graphite and oil-based enamel on paper 46 x 35 in 116.8 x 88.9 cm

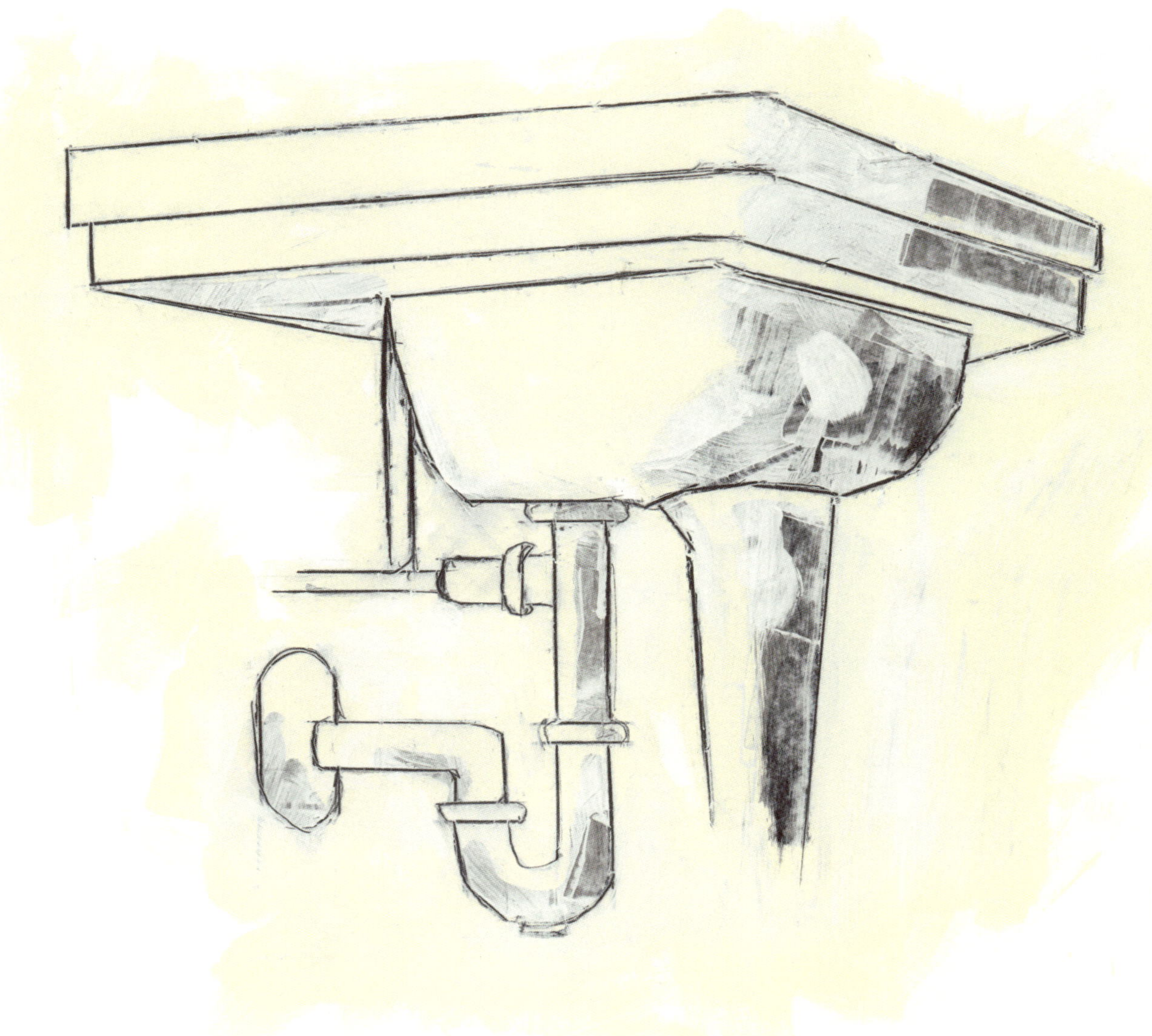

They Work, They Serve 1981 graphite and oil-based enamel on paper 46 x 35 in 116.8 x 88.9 cm

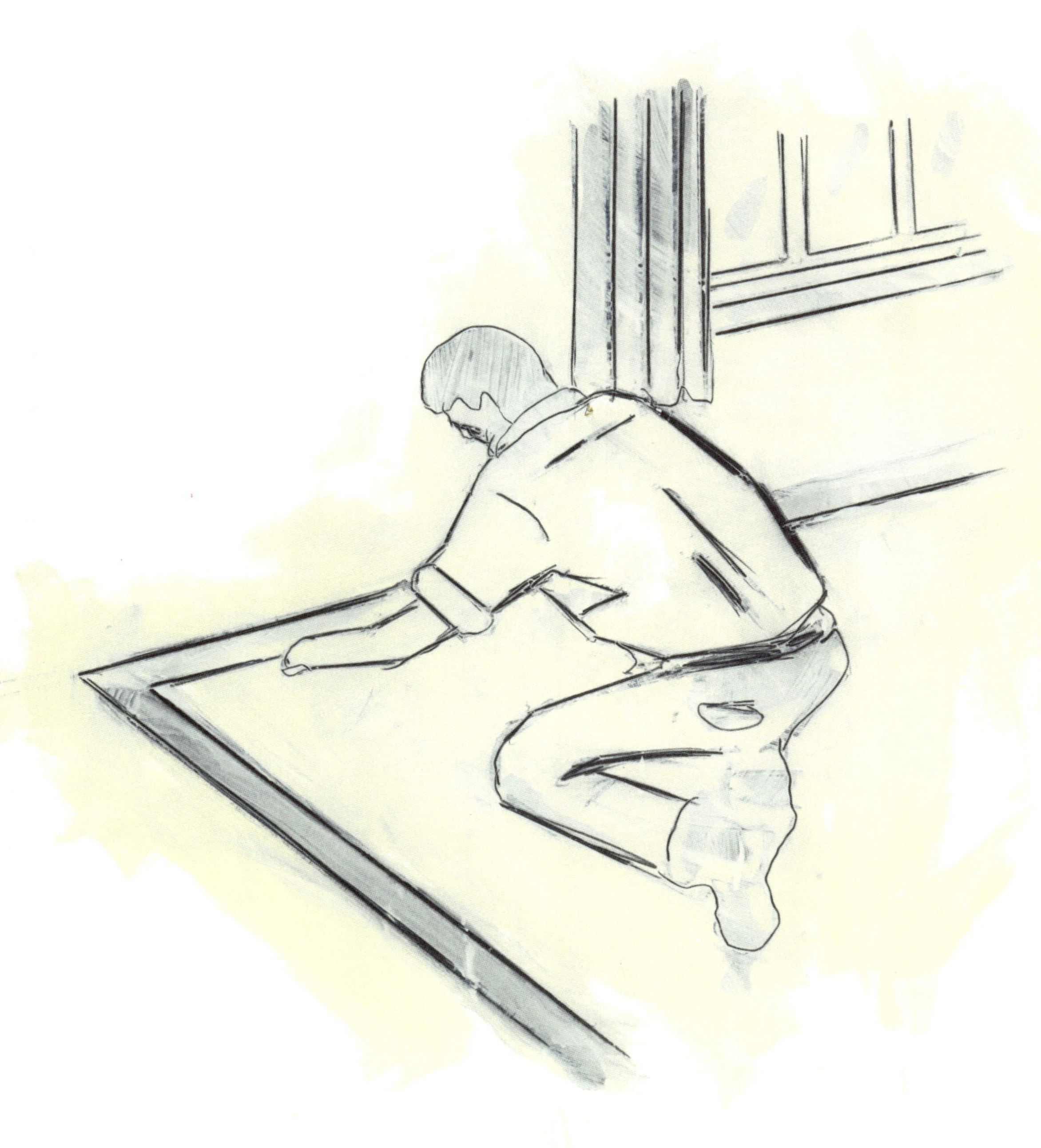

Oum Kalsoum 1981 graphite and oil-based enamel on paper 46 x 35 in 116.8 x 88.9 cm

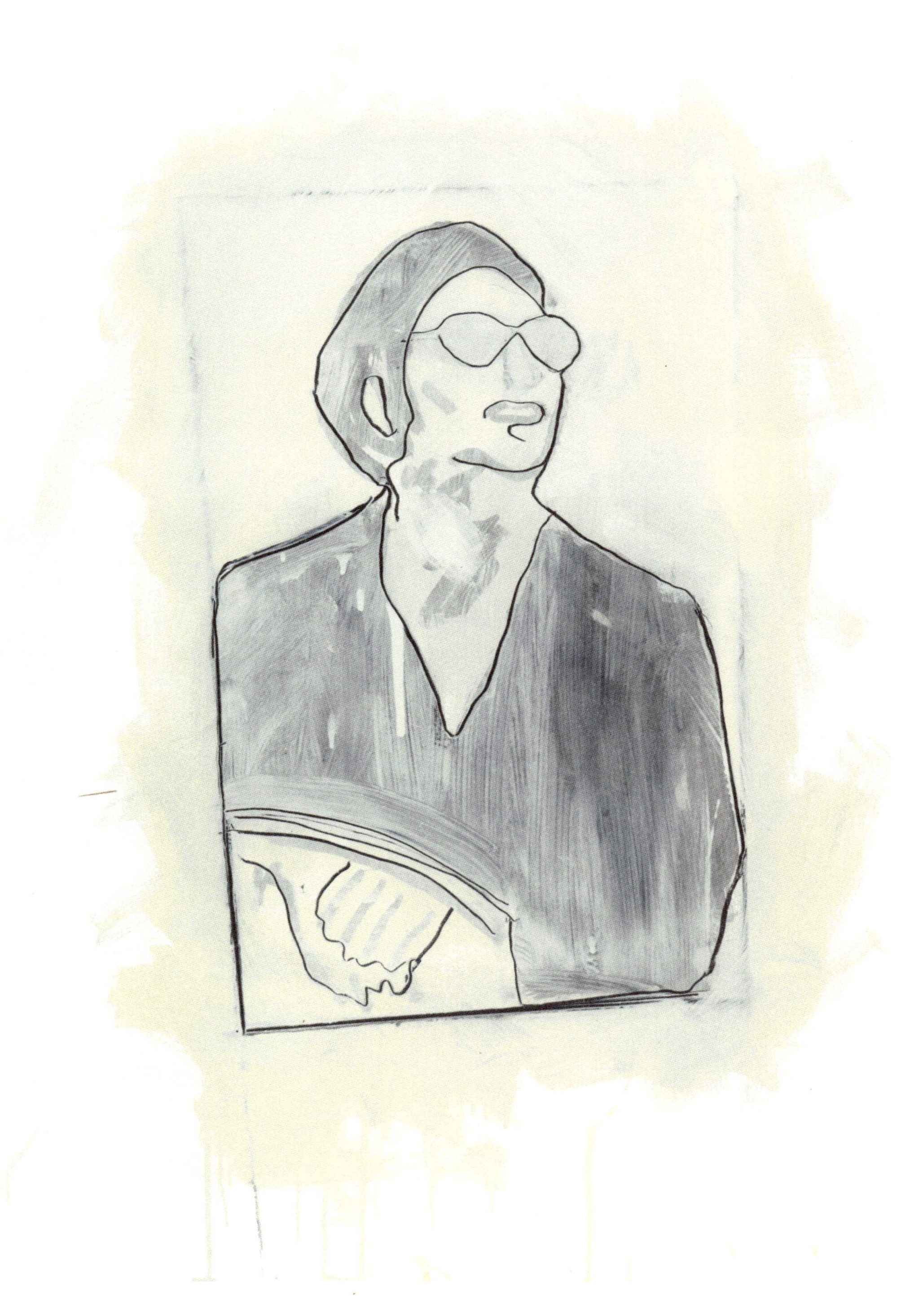

Untitled (Catalog Of Ruins) 1981 graphite and oil-based enamel on paper 46 x 35 in 116.8 x 88.9 cm

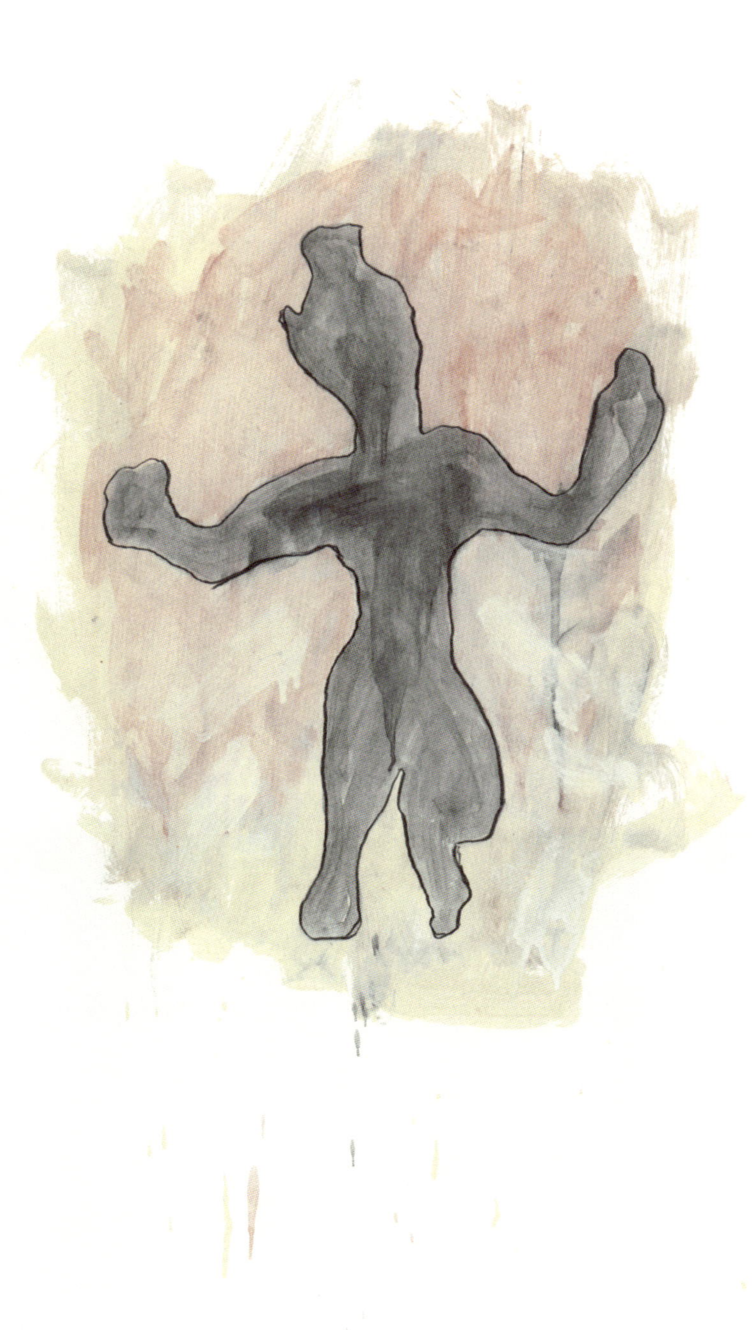

Oum Kalsoum 1981 graphite and oil-based enamel on paper 46 x 35 in 116.8 x 88.9 cm

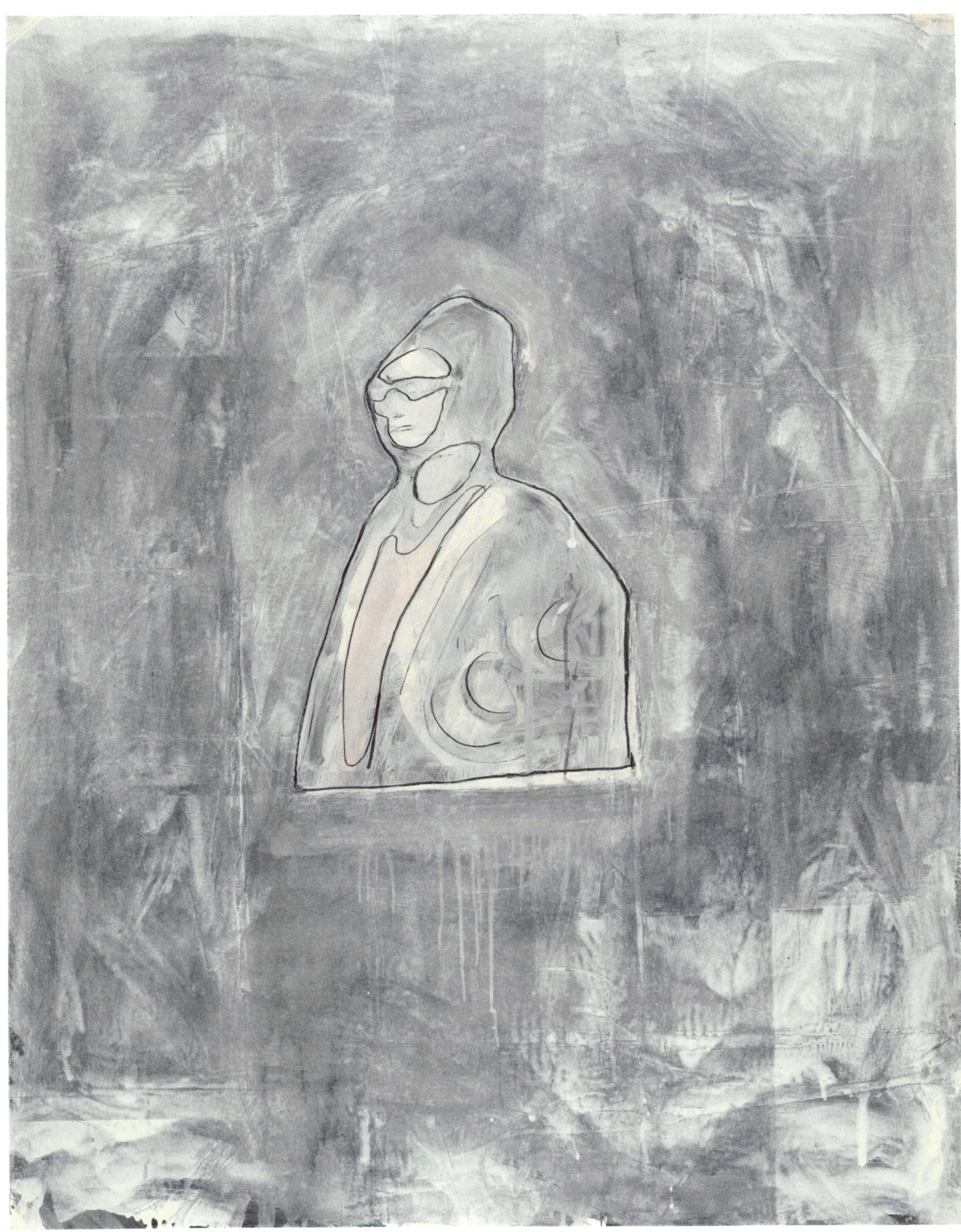

New Iberia 1981 graphite and oil-based enamel on paper 40 x 26 1/4 in 101.6 x 66.7 cm

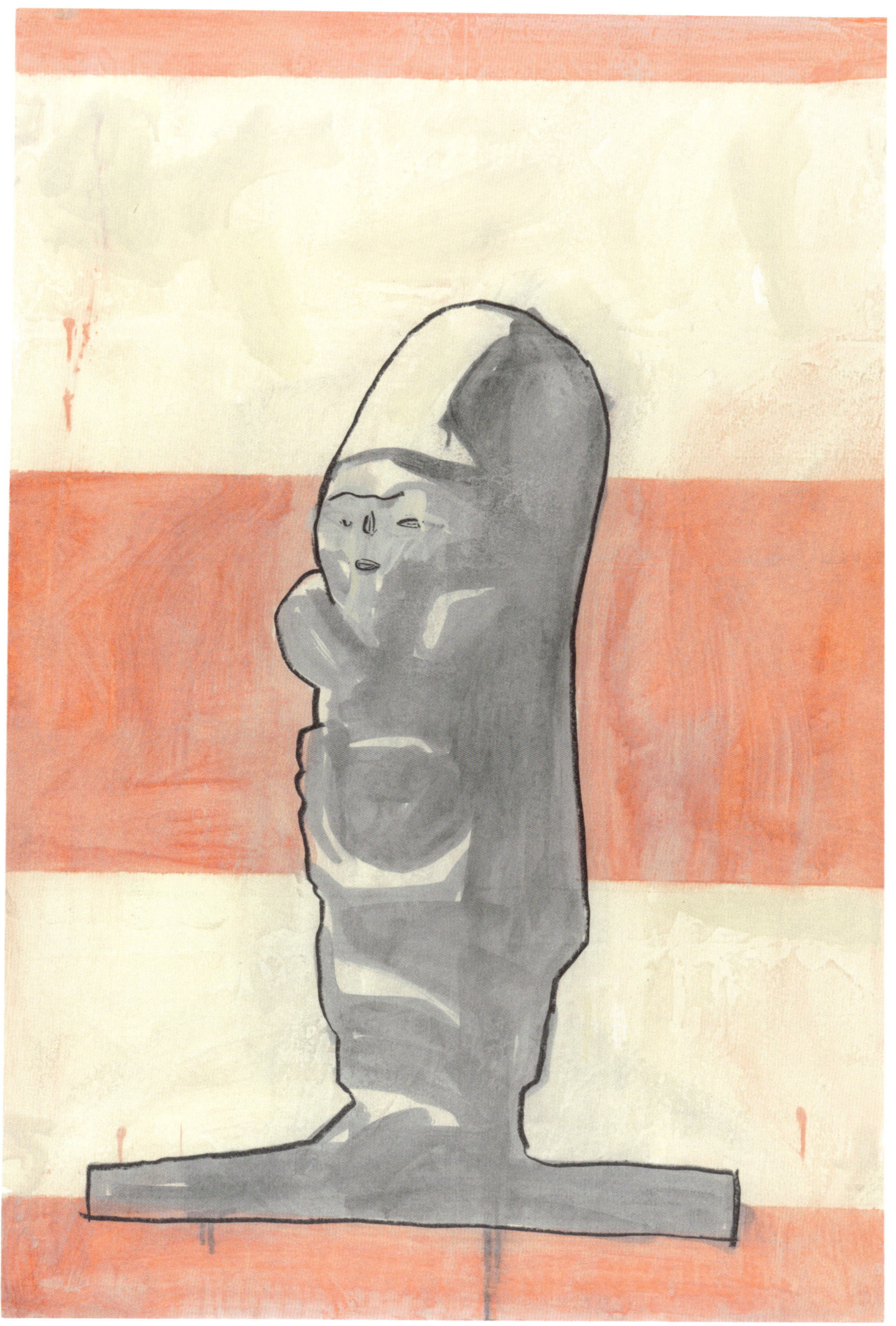

New Iberia 1981 graphite and oil-based enamel on paper 40 x 26 in 101.6 x 66 cm

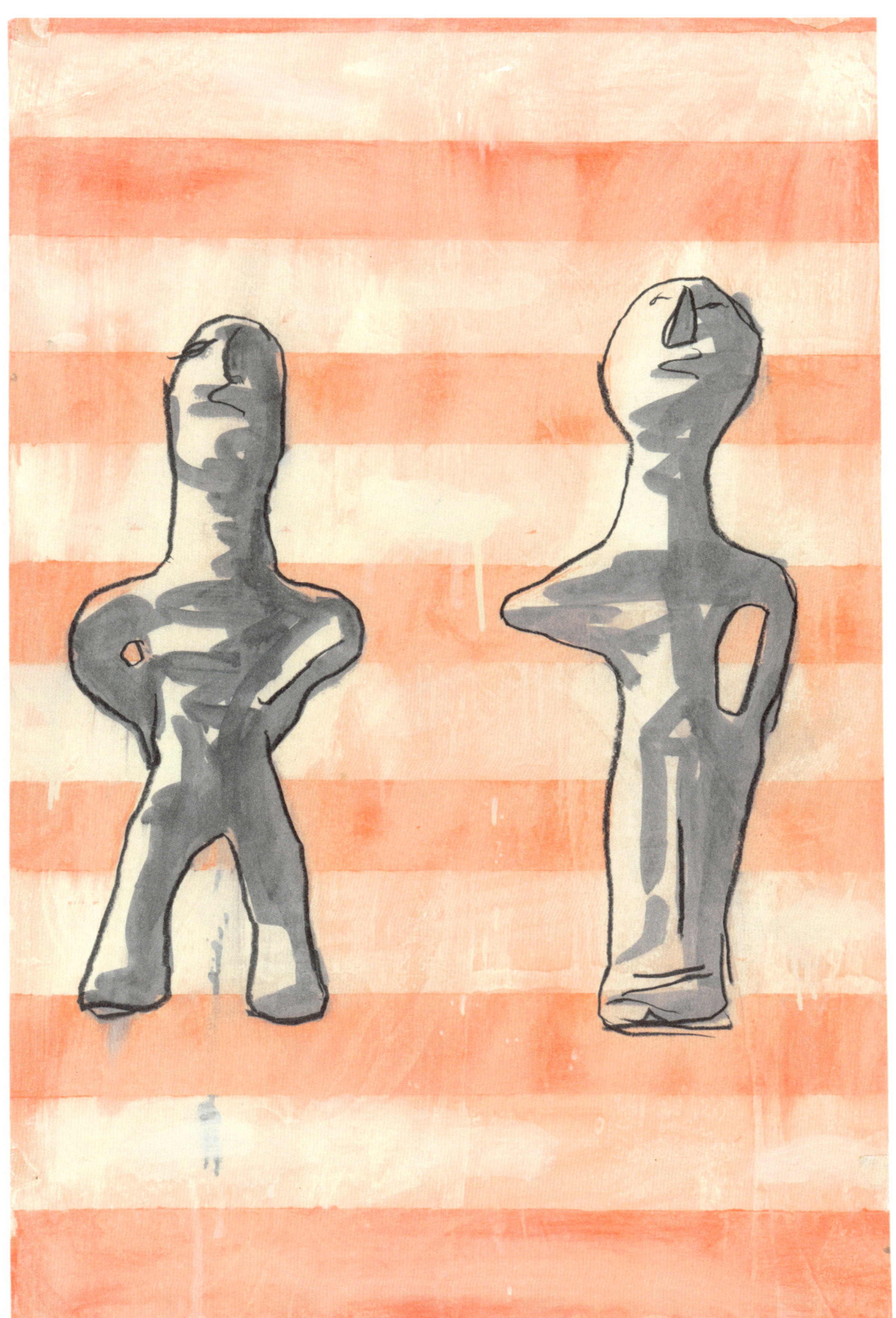

Pair 1981 graphite and oil-based enamel on paper 26 x 26 in 66 x 66 cm

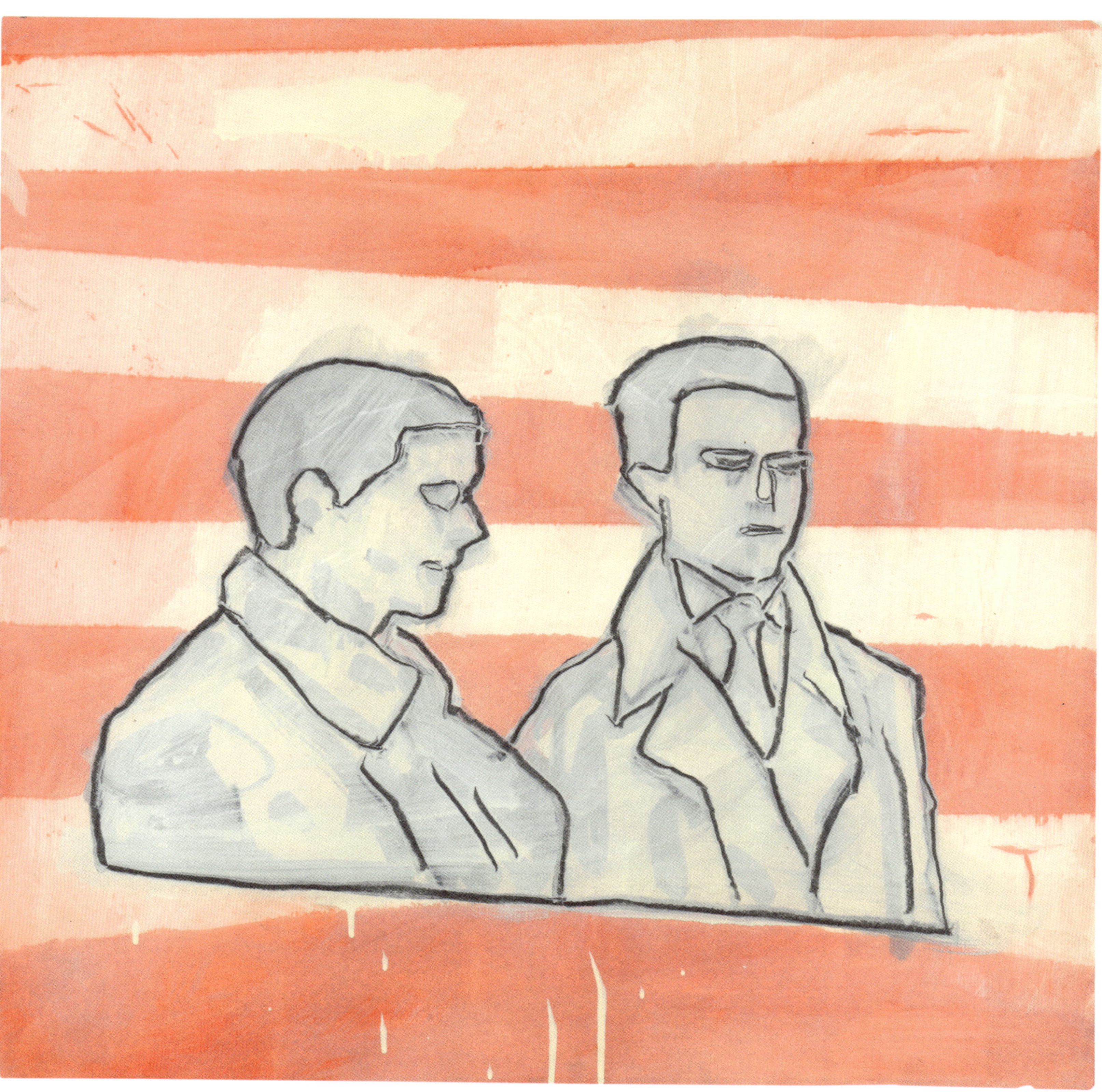

Three Figures (Wall Street Week) 1981 graphite, spray enamel and oil-based enamel on paper 18 x 18 in 45.7 x 45.7 cm

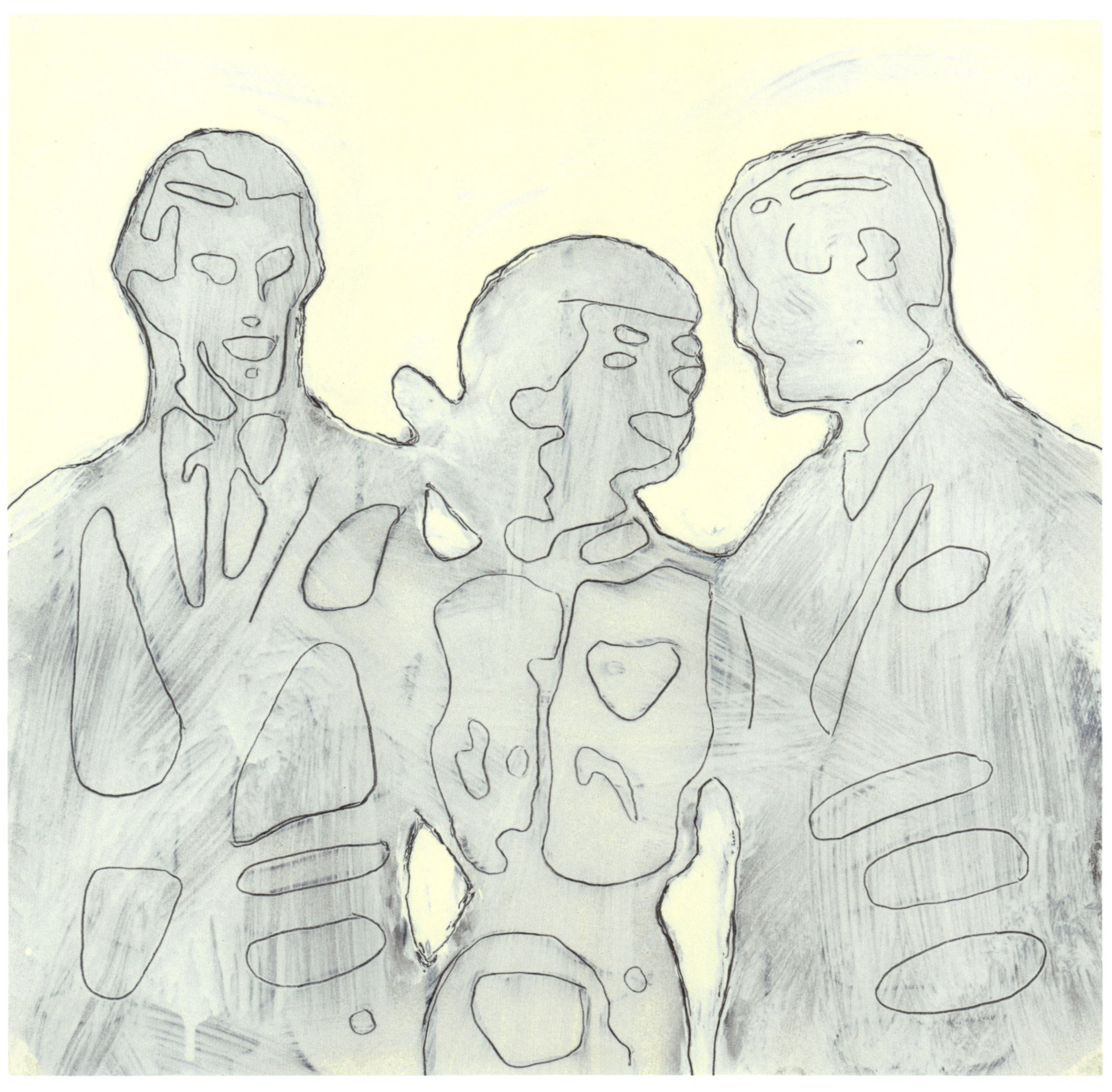

Resort Group (Food) Second Version 1982 oil based enamel on paper 46 x 35 in 116.8 x 88.9 cm

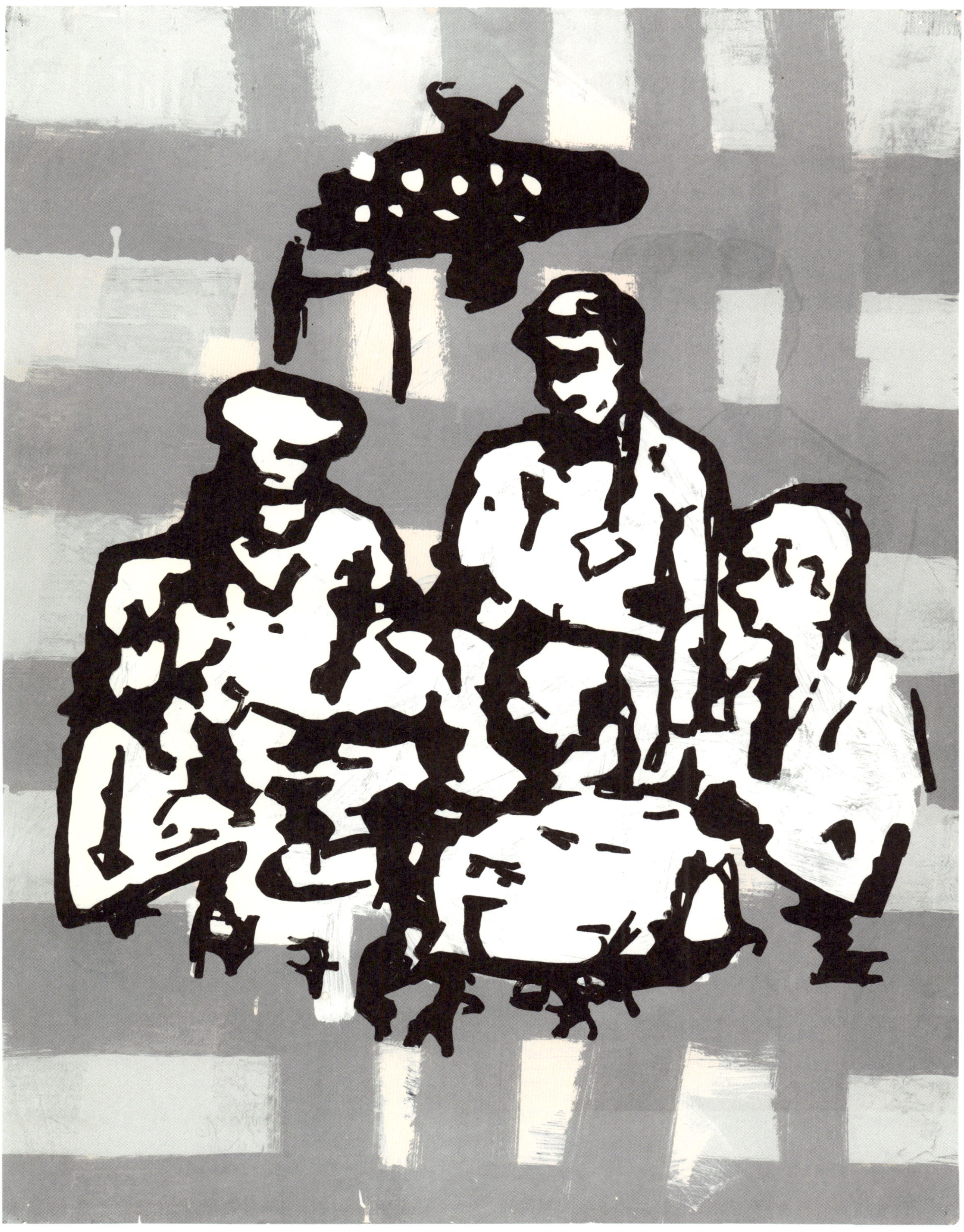

Untitled (Study for Portrait of Antinous) 1982 oil based enamel on paper 46 x 35 in 116.8 x 88.9 cm

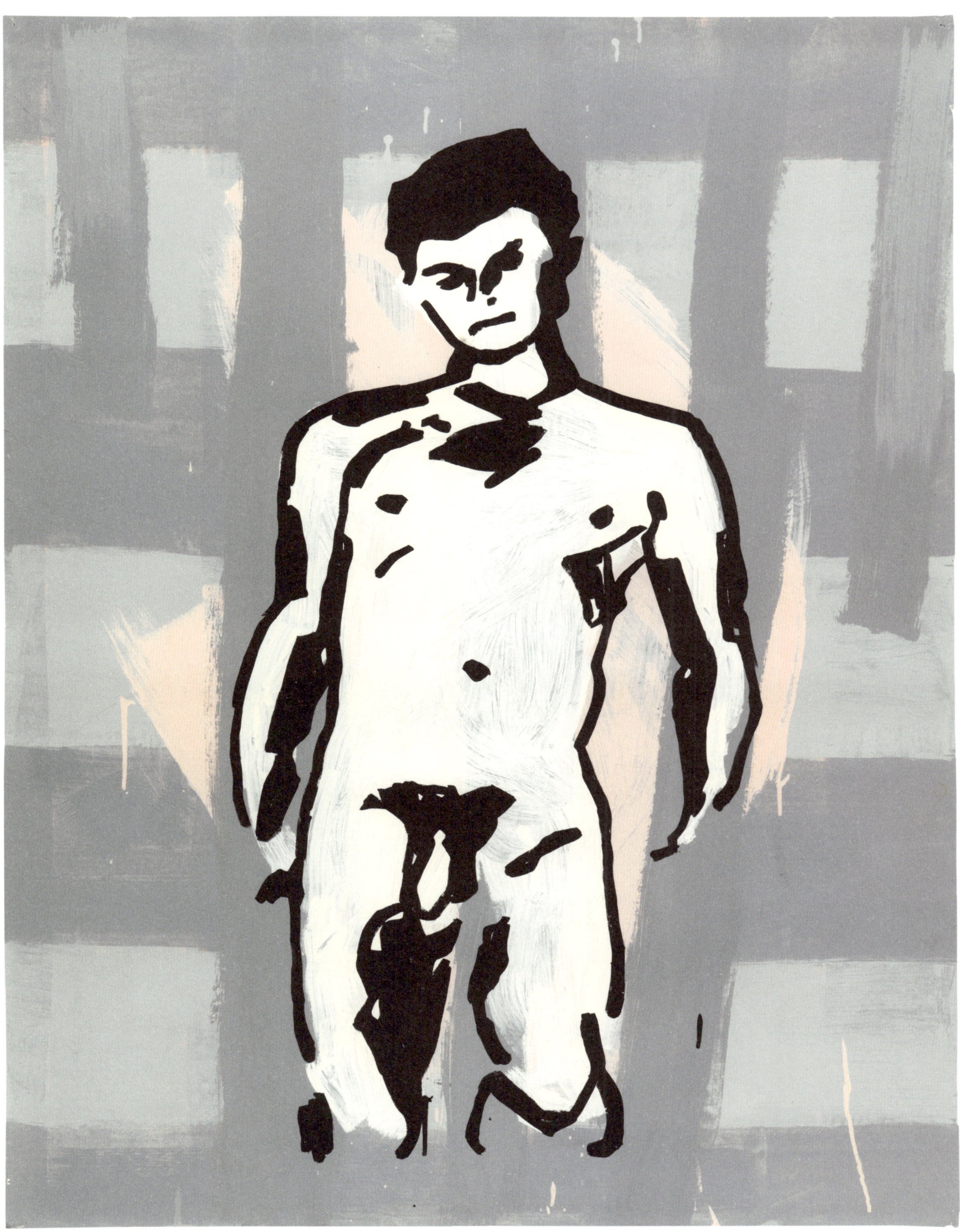

Untitled 1982 oil based enamel on paper 46 x 35 in 116.8 x 88.9 cm

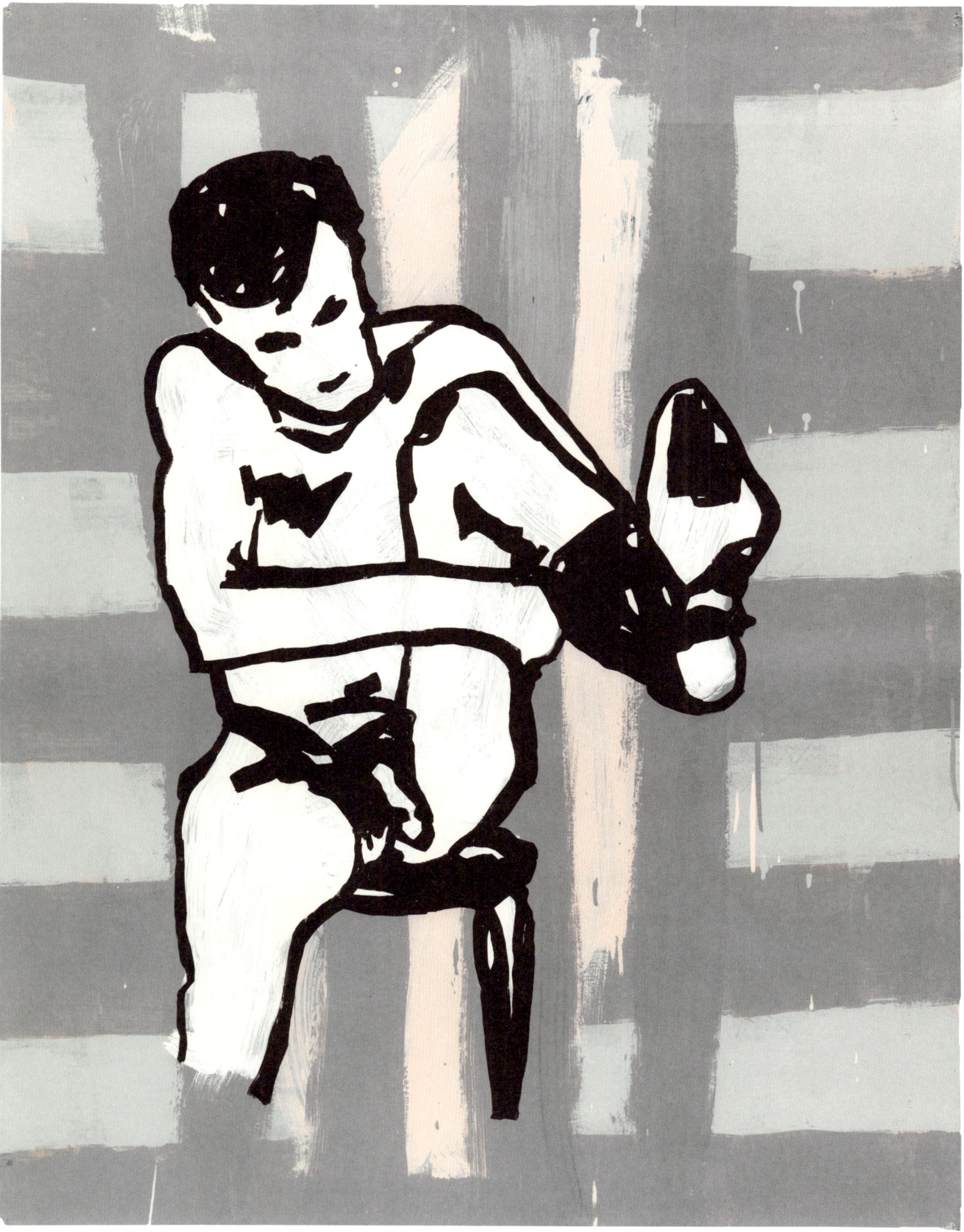

Figure Study (Shelby Creagh) 1982 acrylic, graphite and muslin collage on paper 40 x 32 in 101.6 x 81.3 cm

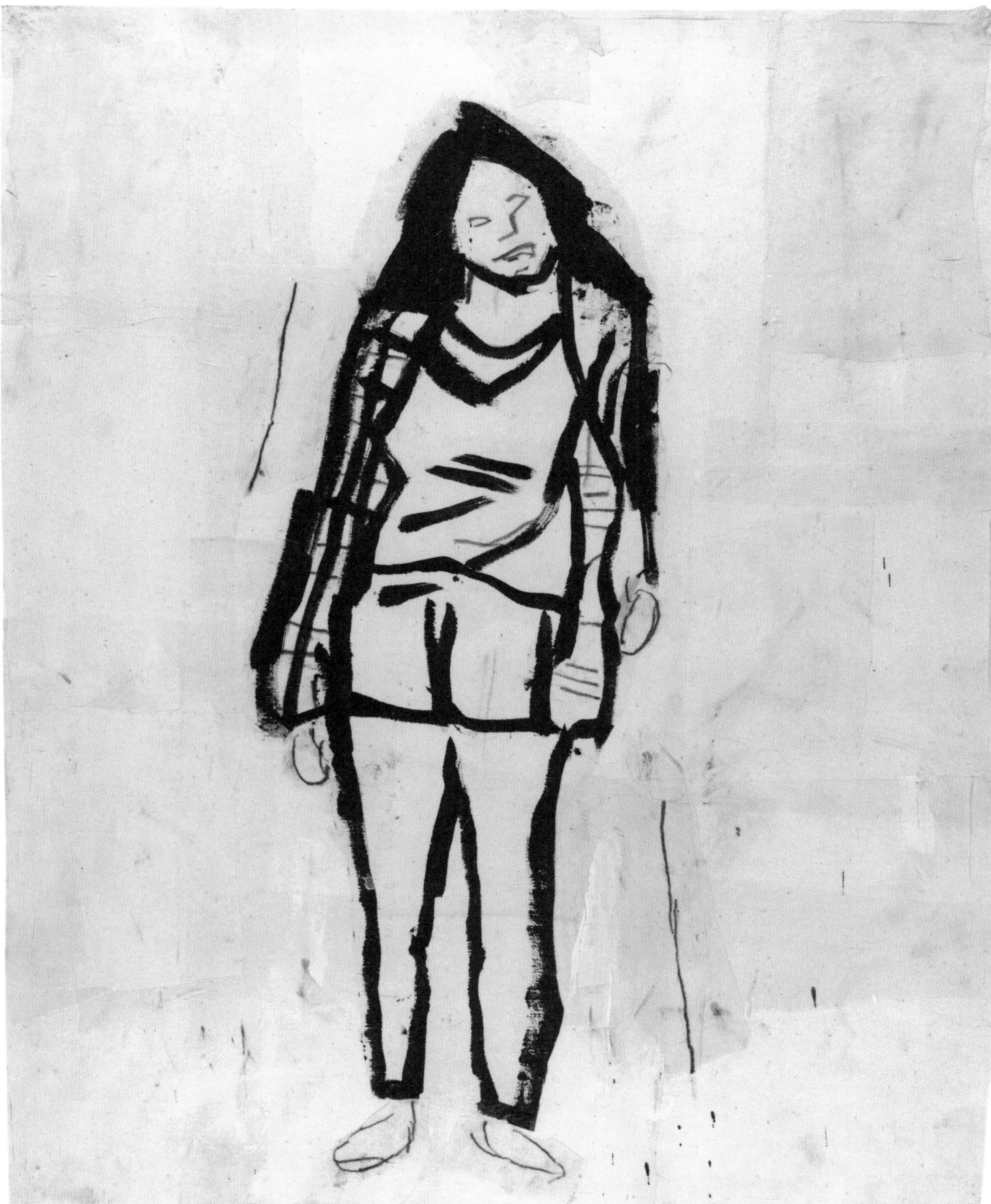

Figure Study #2 1982 acrylic, graphite and muslin collage on paper 40 x 32 in 101.6 x 81.3 cm

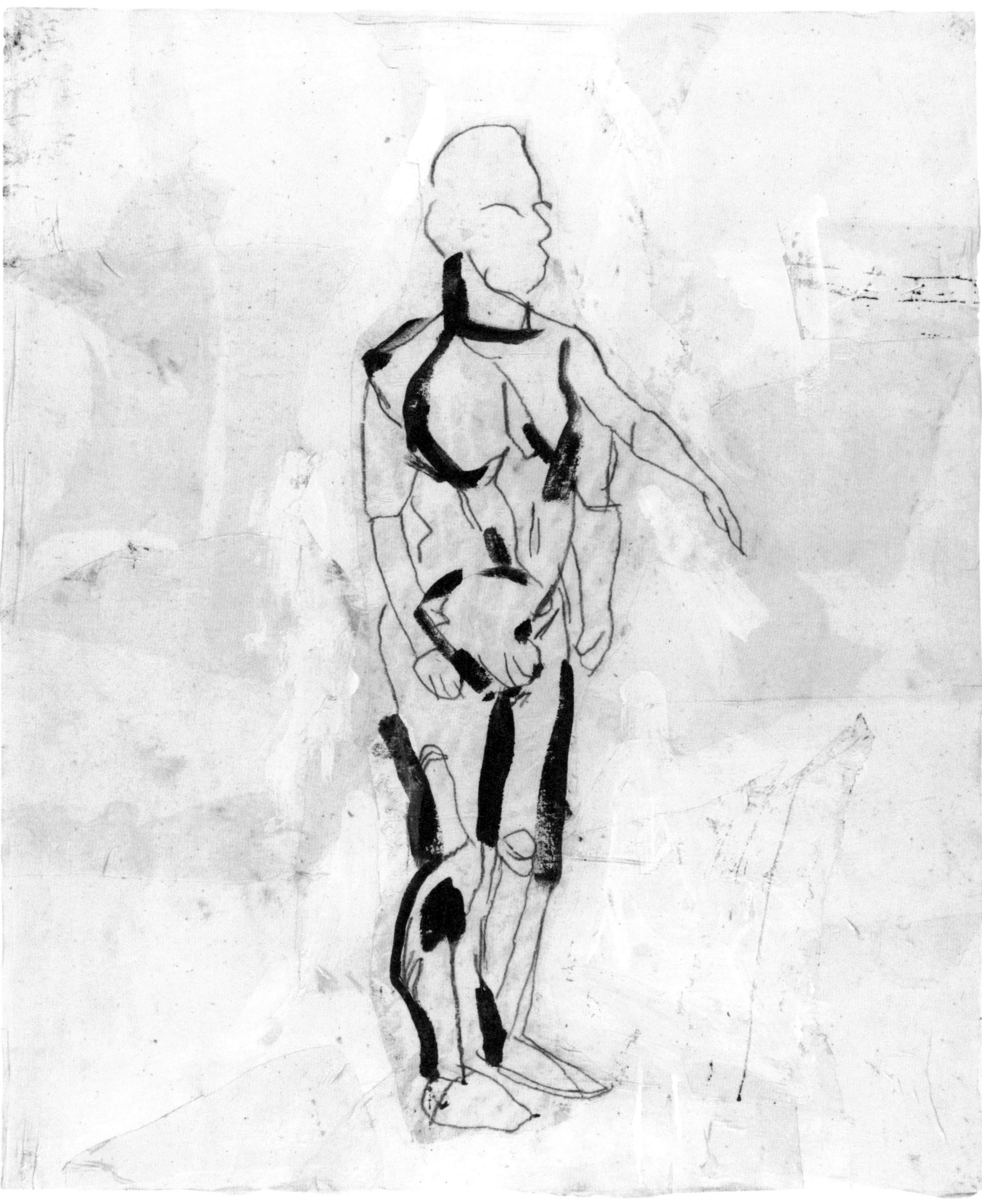

Figure Study #3 1982 acrylic, graphite and muslin collage on paper 40 x 32 in 101.6 x 81.3 cm

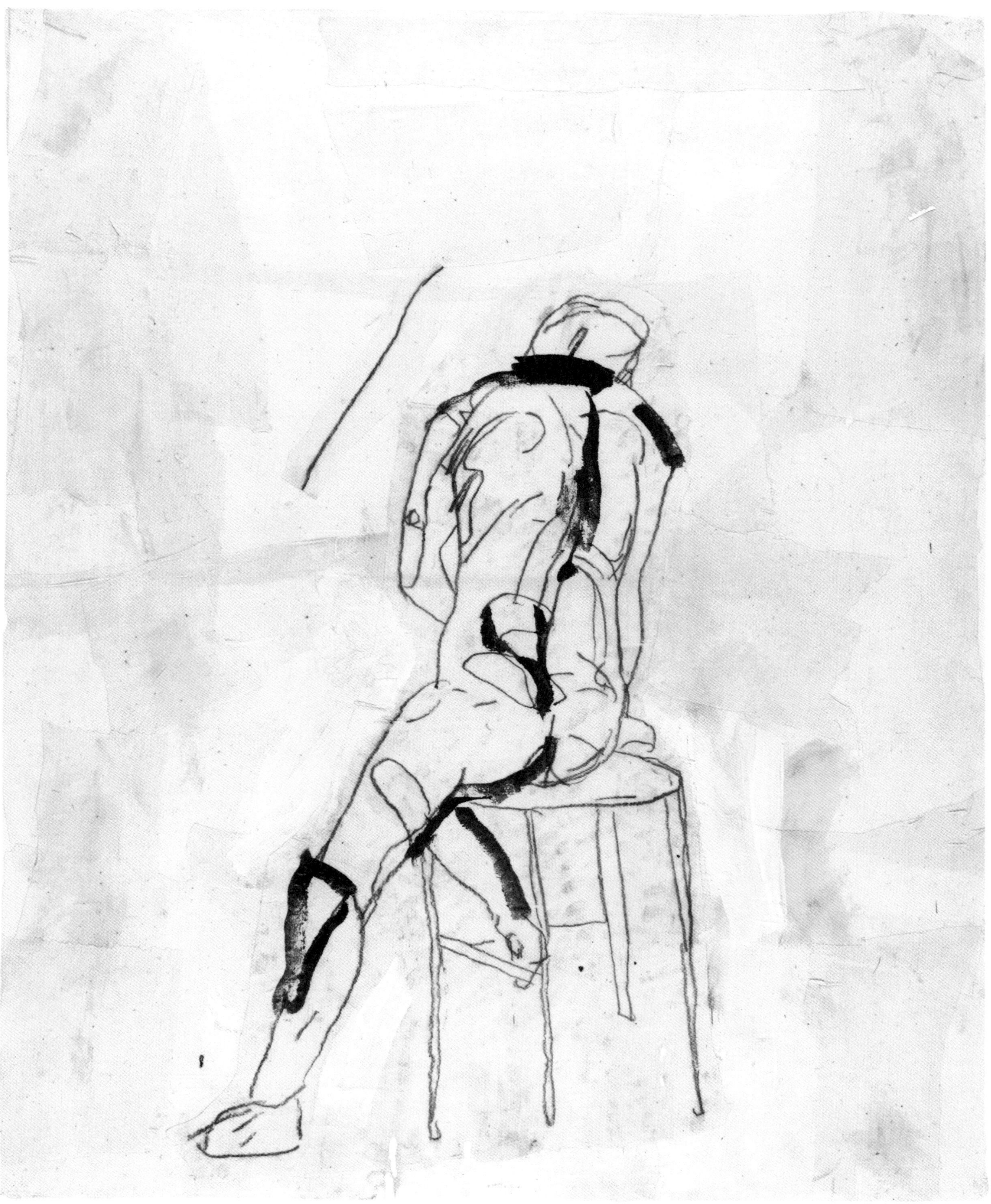

Figure Study #1 1982 acrylic, graphite and muslin collage on paper 40 x 32 in 101.6 x 81.3 cm

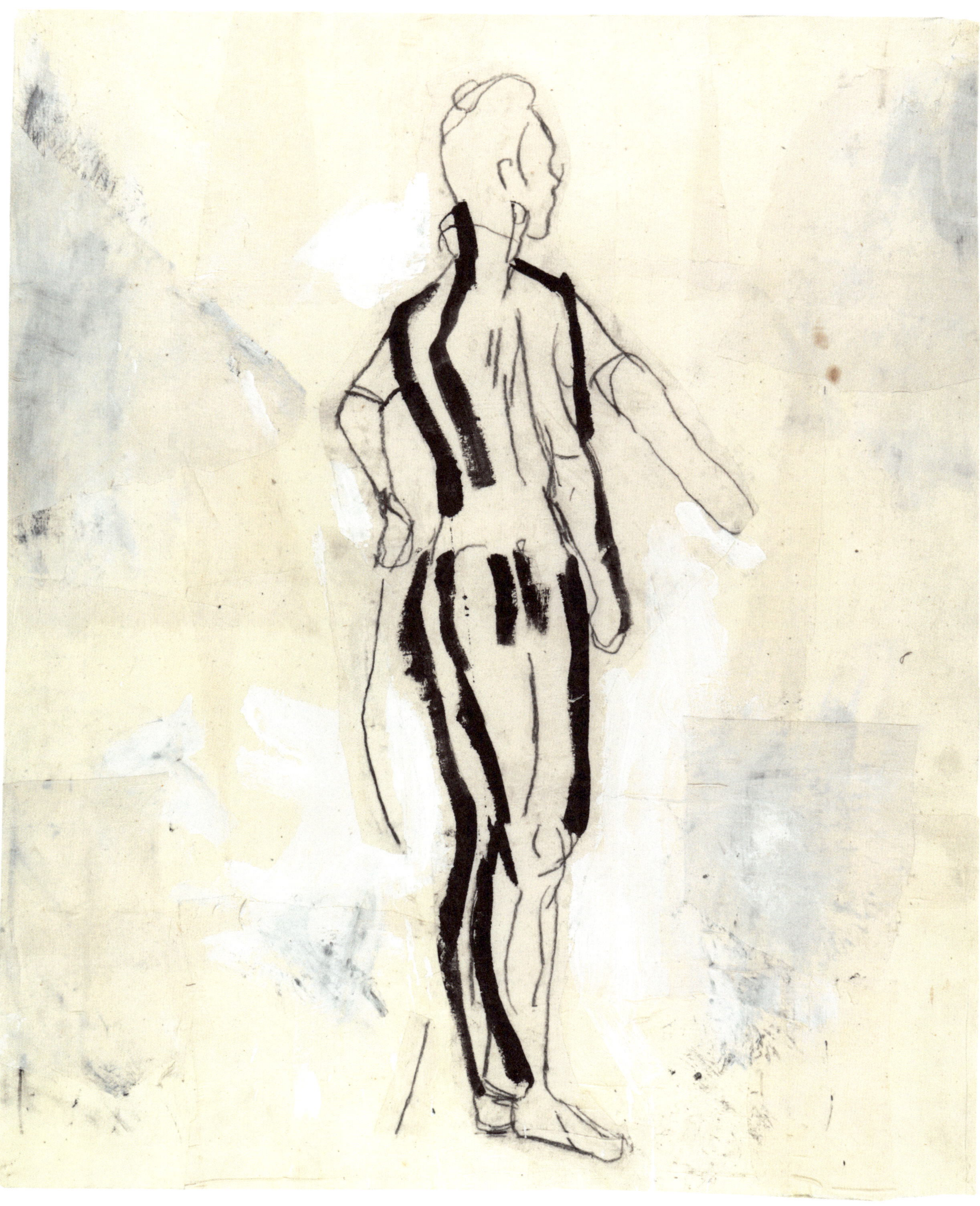

Reclining Nude (After Shelby Creagh) 1982 acrylic, graphite and muslin collage on paper 40 x 32 in 101.6 x 81.3 cm

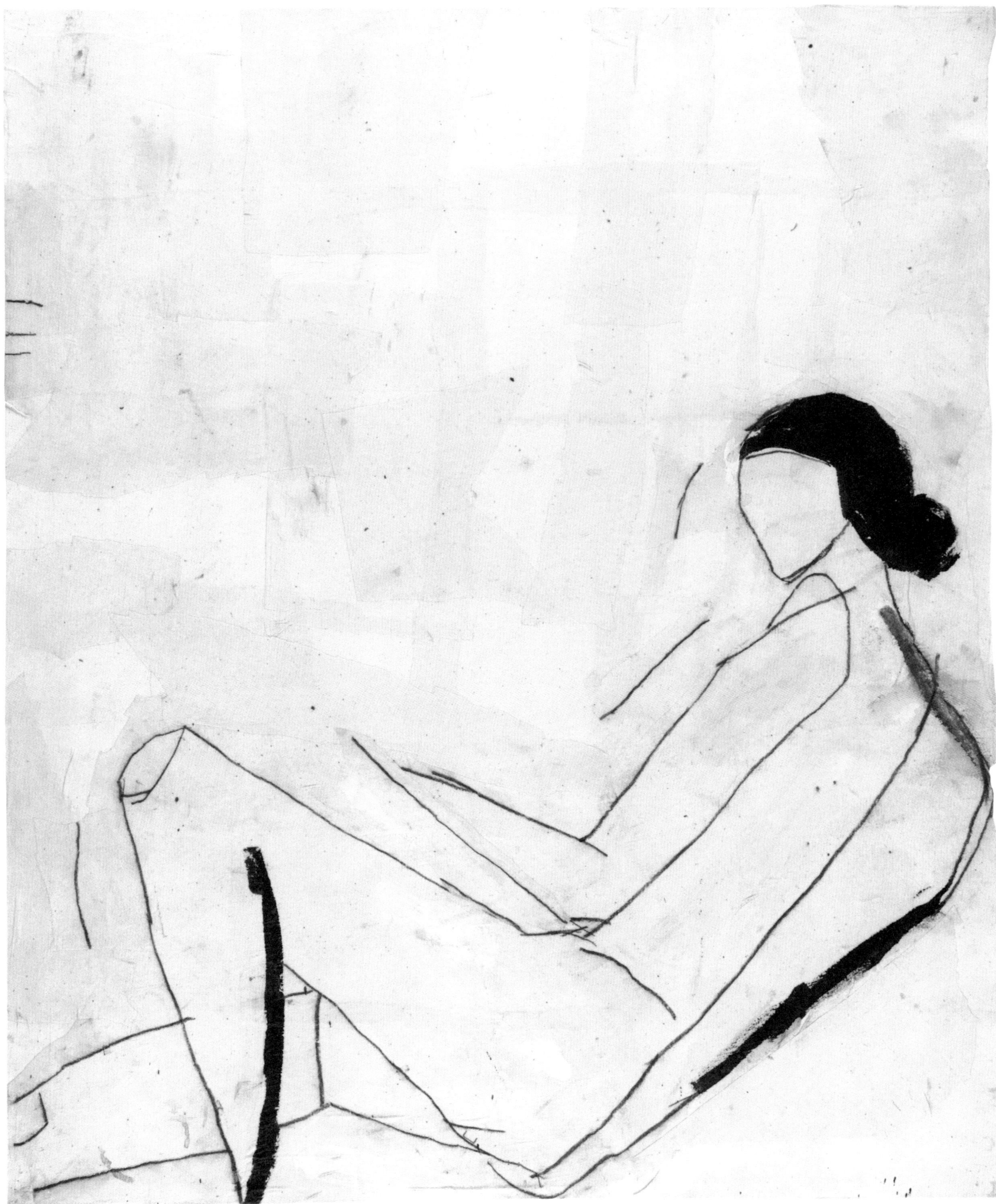

Standing Nude (After Shelby Creagh) 1982 acrylic, graphite and muslin collage on paper 40 x 32 in 101.6 x 81.3 cm

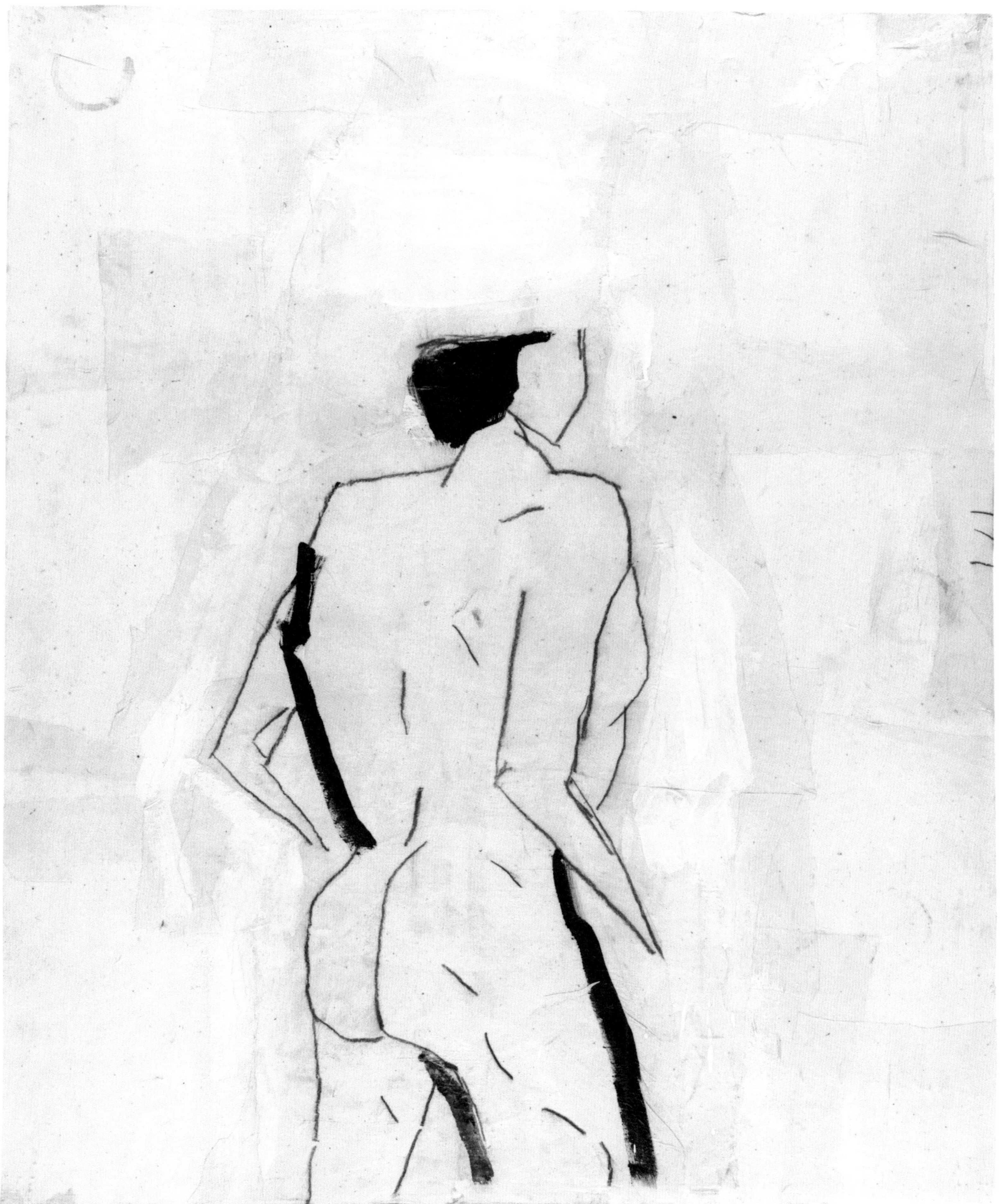

**Fists of Fury 1983 acrylic, tempera, graphite and paper collage on paper 36 x 36 in 91.4 x 91.4 cm

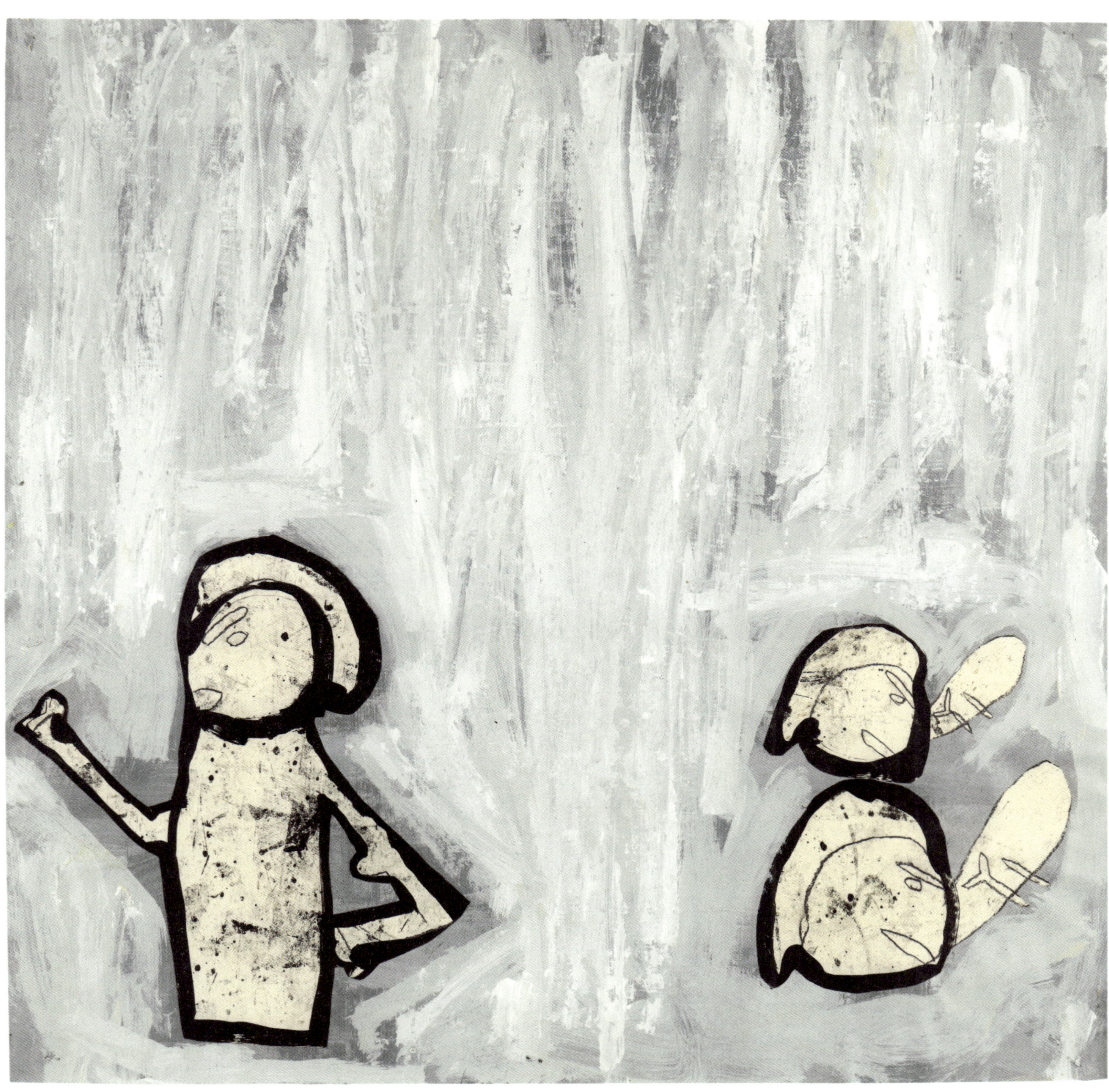

**Fists of Fury 1983 acrylic, tempera, graphite and paper collage on paper 42 x 42 in 106.7 x 106.7 cm

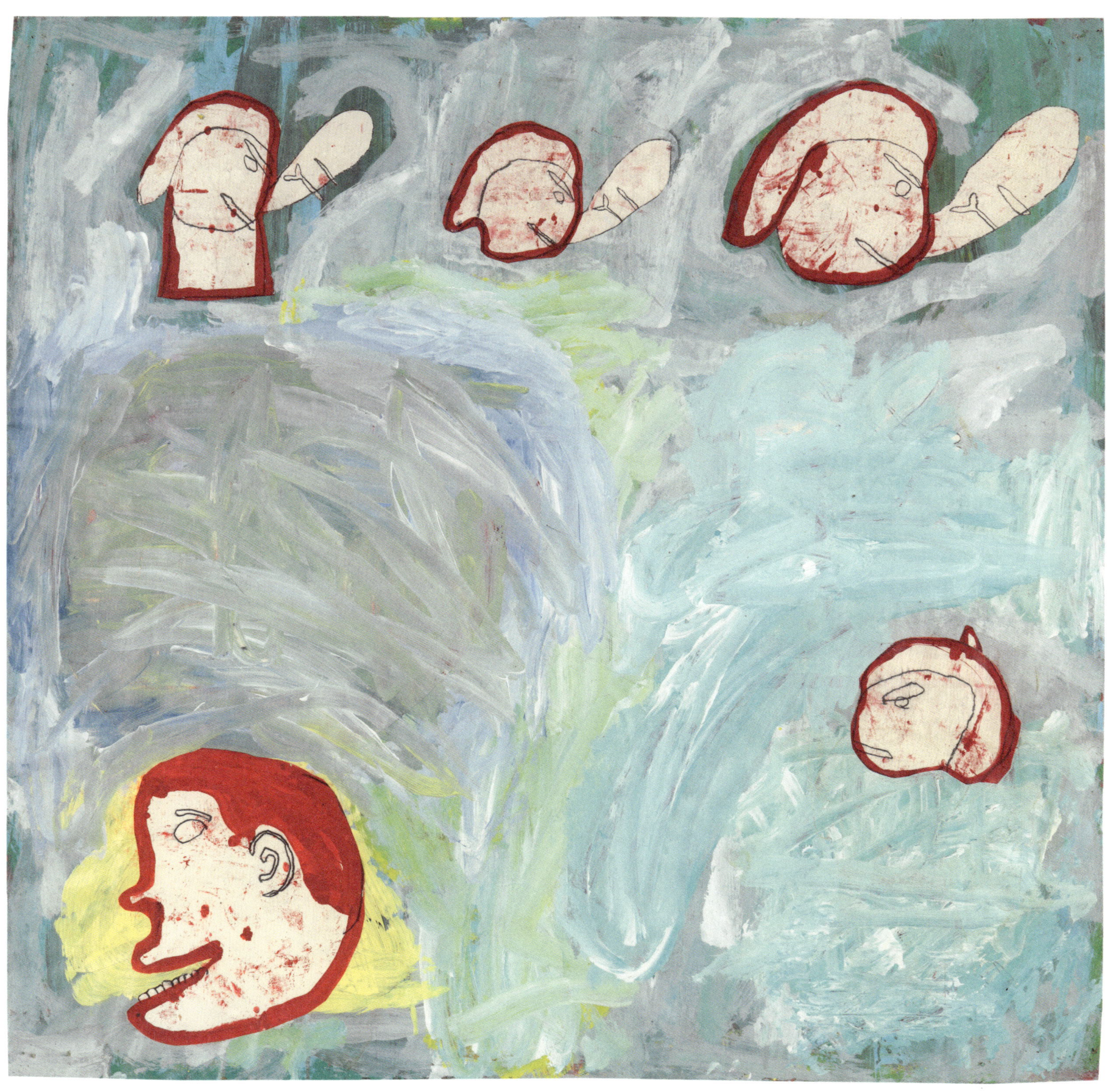

Untitled 1983 acrylic, tempera, graphite and paper collage on paper 42 x 42 in 106.7 x 106.7 cm

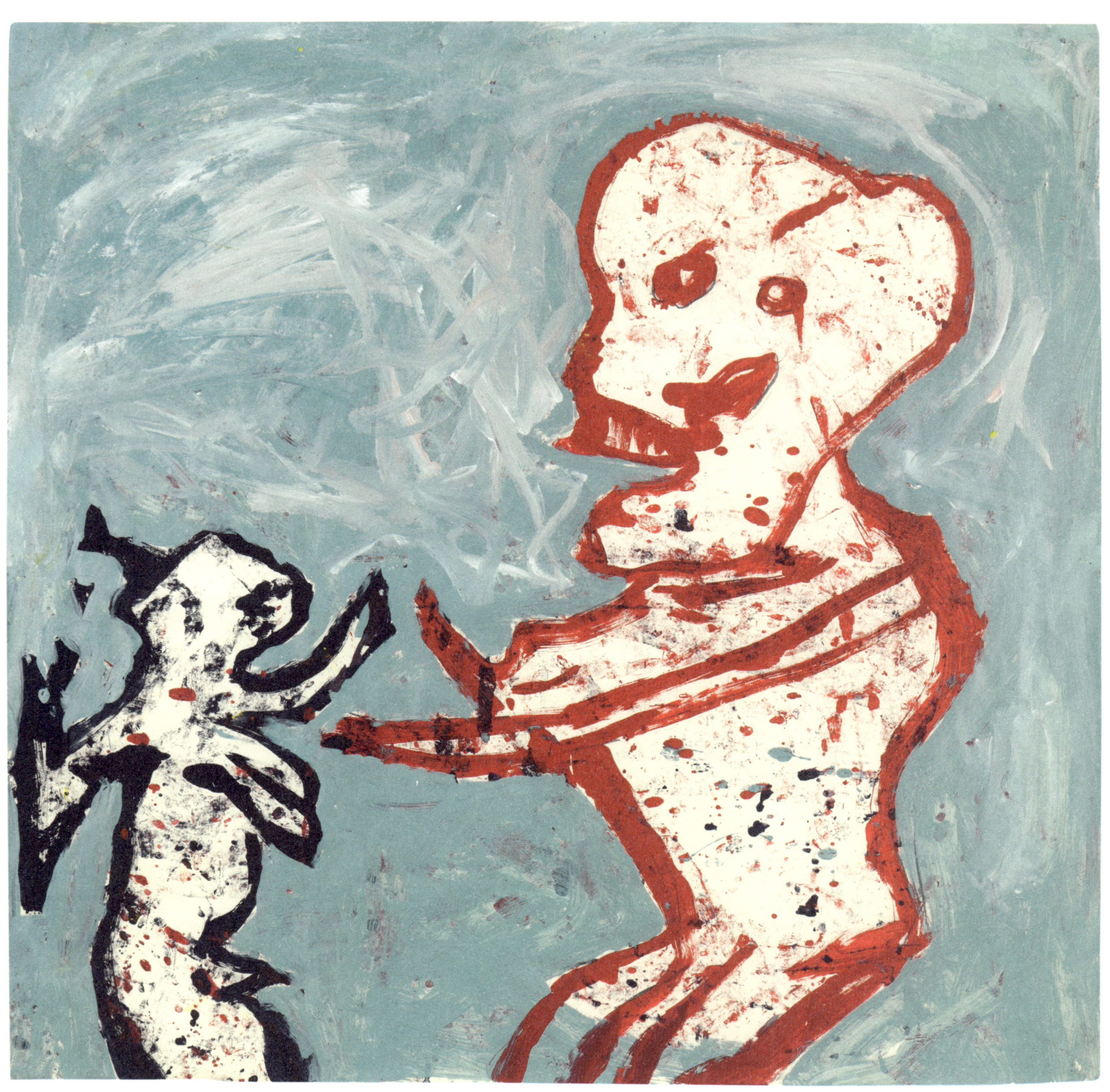

Fists of Fury 1983 acrylic, tempera, graphite and paper collage on paper 42 x 42 in 106.7 x 106.7 cm

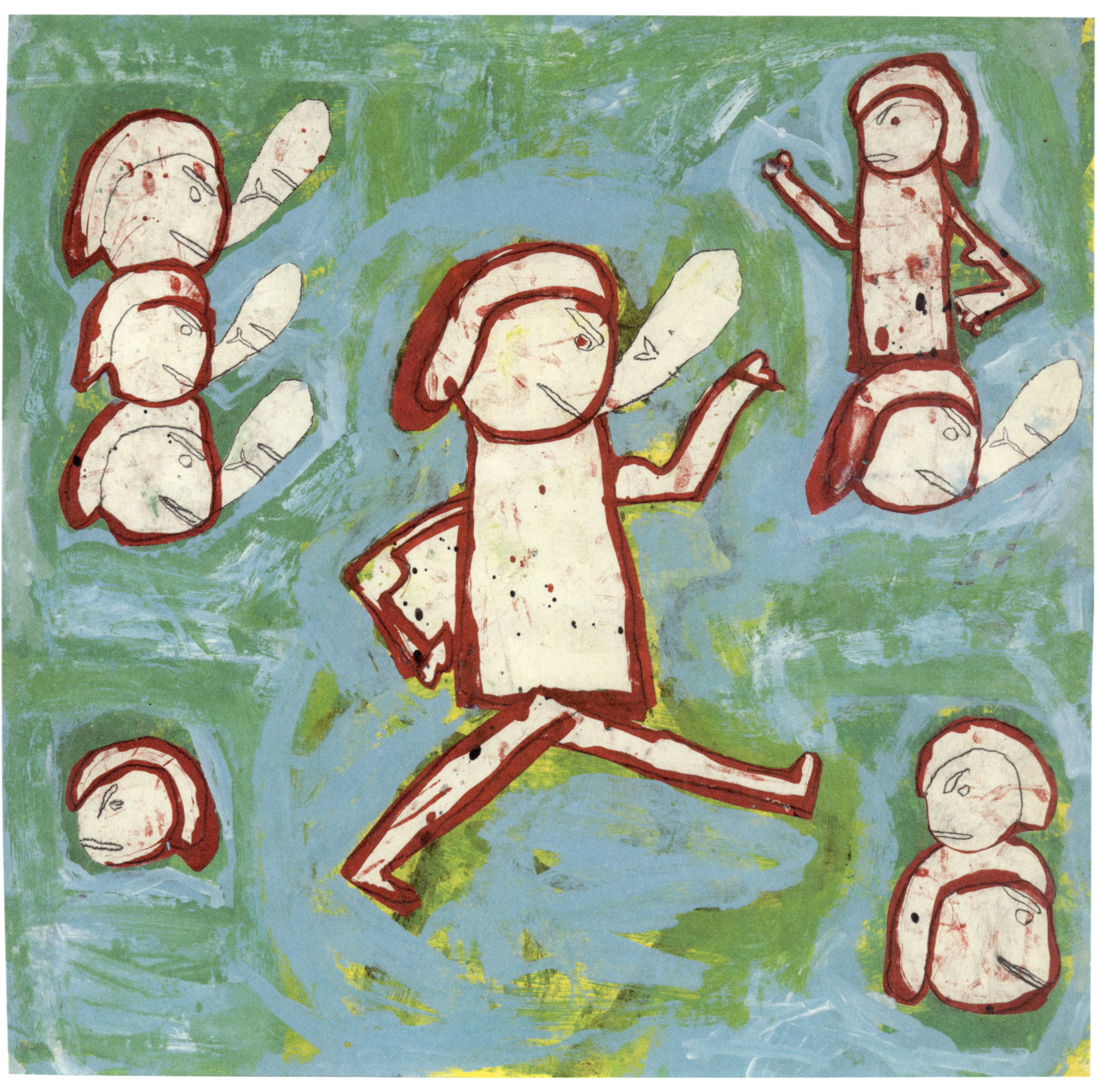

Fists of Fury 1983 acrylic, tempera, graphite and paper collage on paper 42 x 42 in 106.7 x 106.7 cm

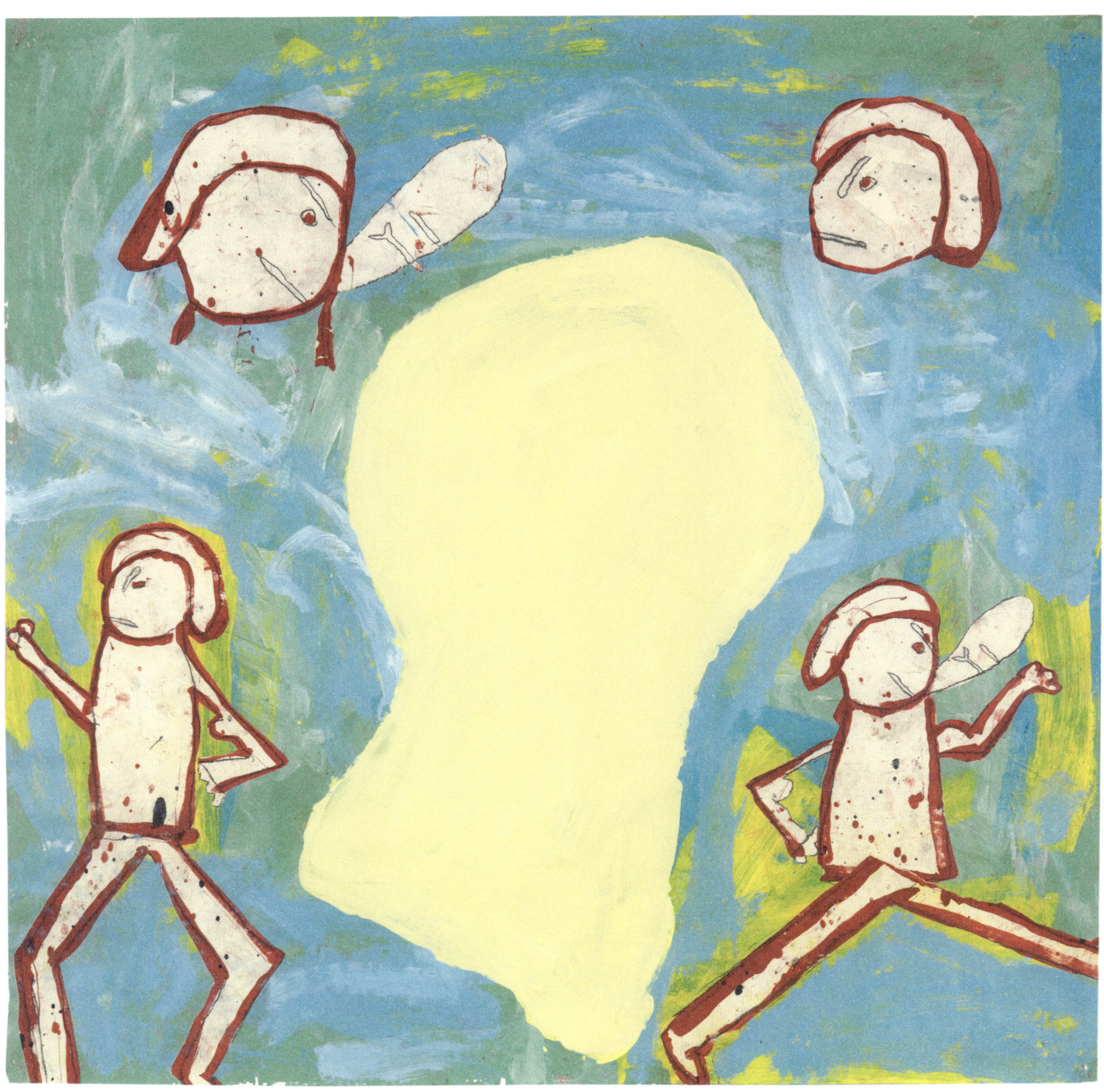

Spiral Head 1983 graphite, tempera and paper collage on paper 42 x 42 in 106.7 x 106.7 cm

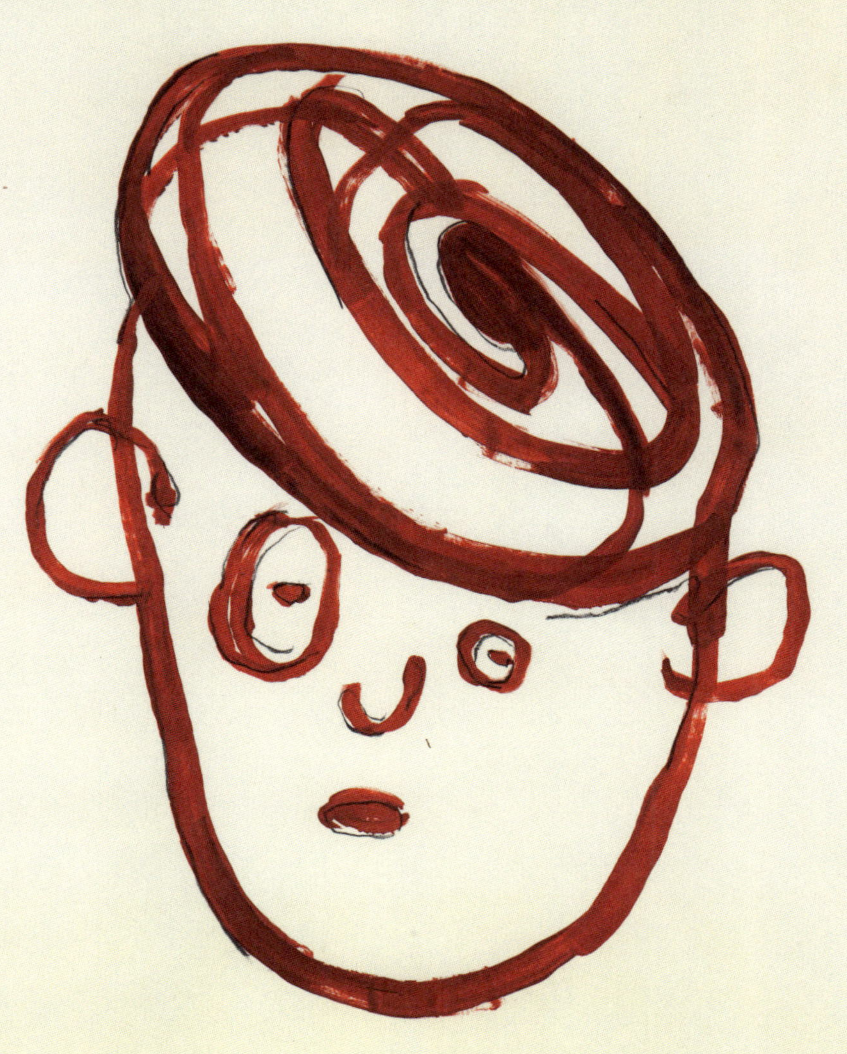

Untitled (Spiral Head) 1983 graphite, tempera and paper collage on paper 42 x 42 in 106.7 x 106.7 cm

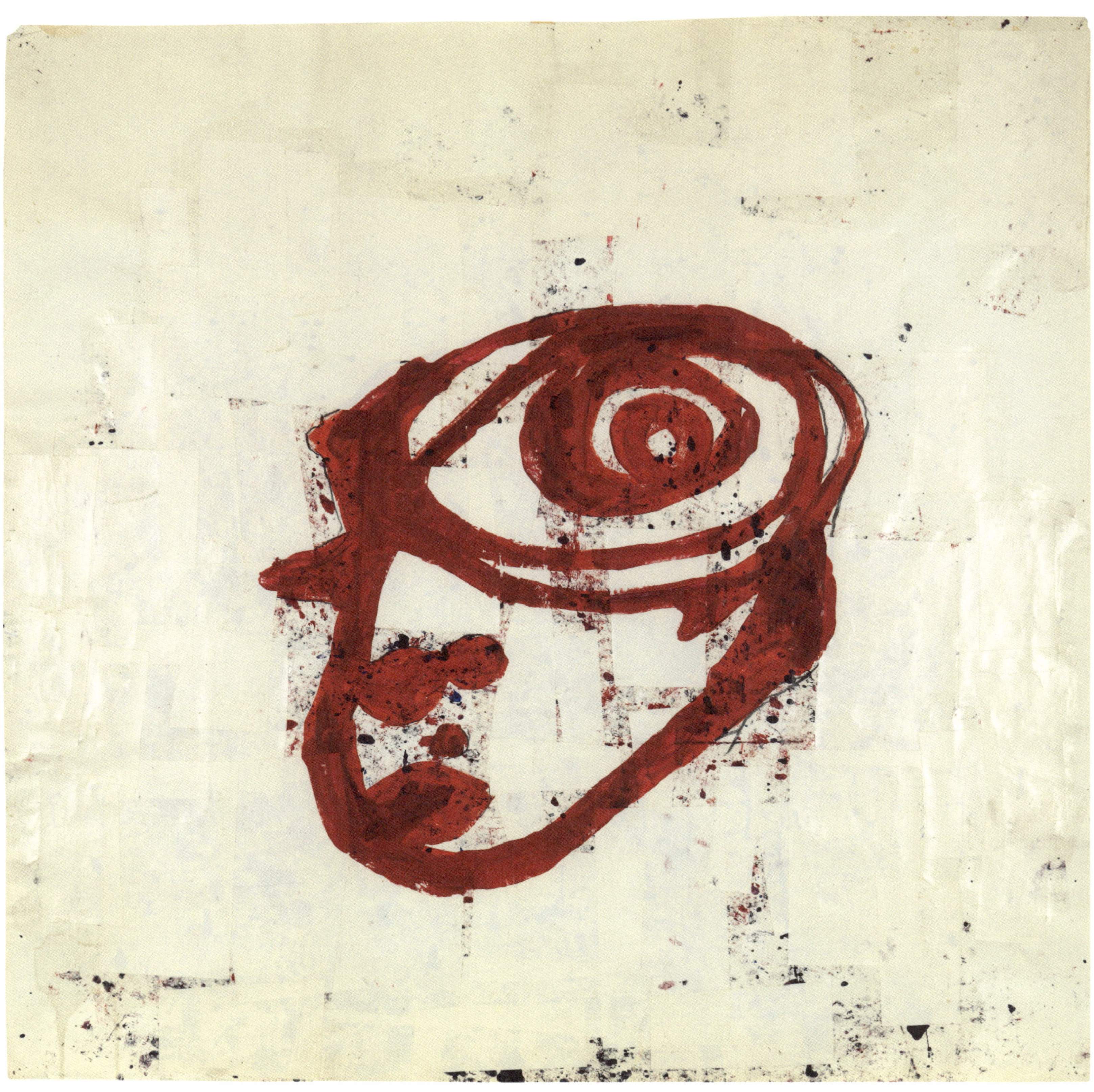

Fists of Fury 1983 acrylic, tempera, graphite and paper collage on paper 36 x 36 in 91.4 x 91.4 cm

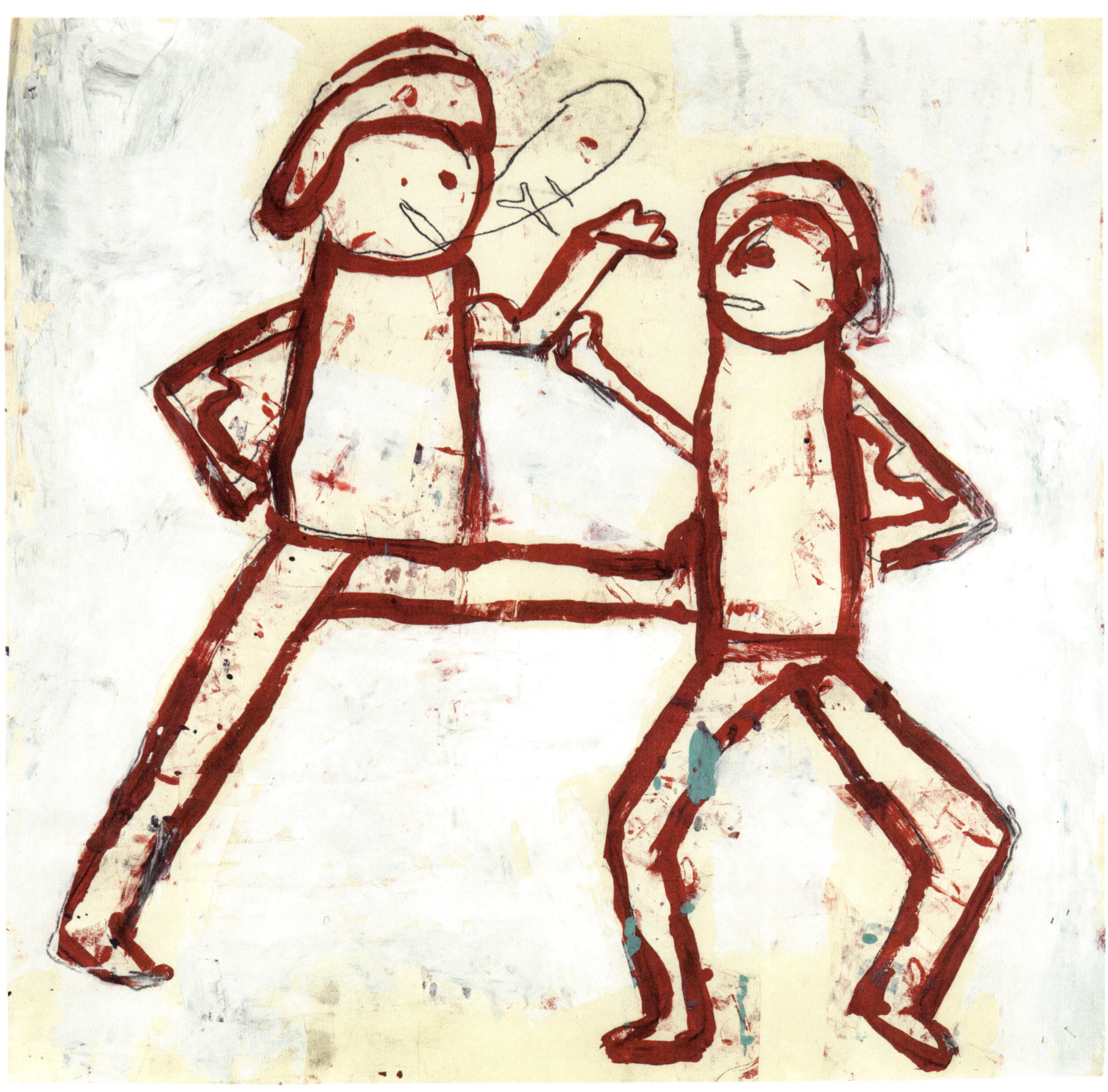

Girl and Bather 1983 acrylic, tempera, graphite and paper collage on paper 36 x 36 in 91.4 x 91.4 cm

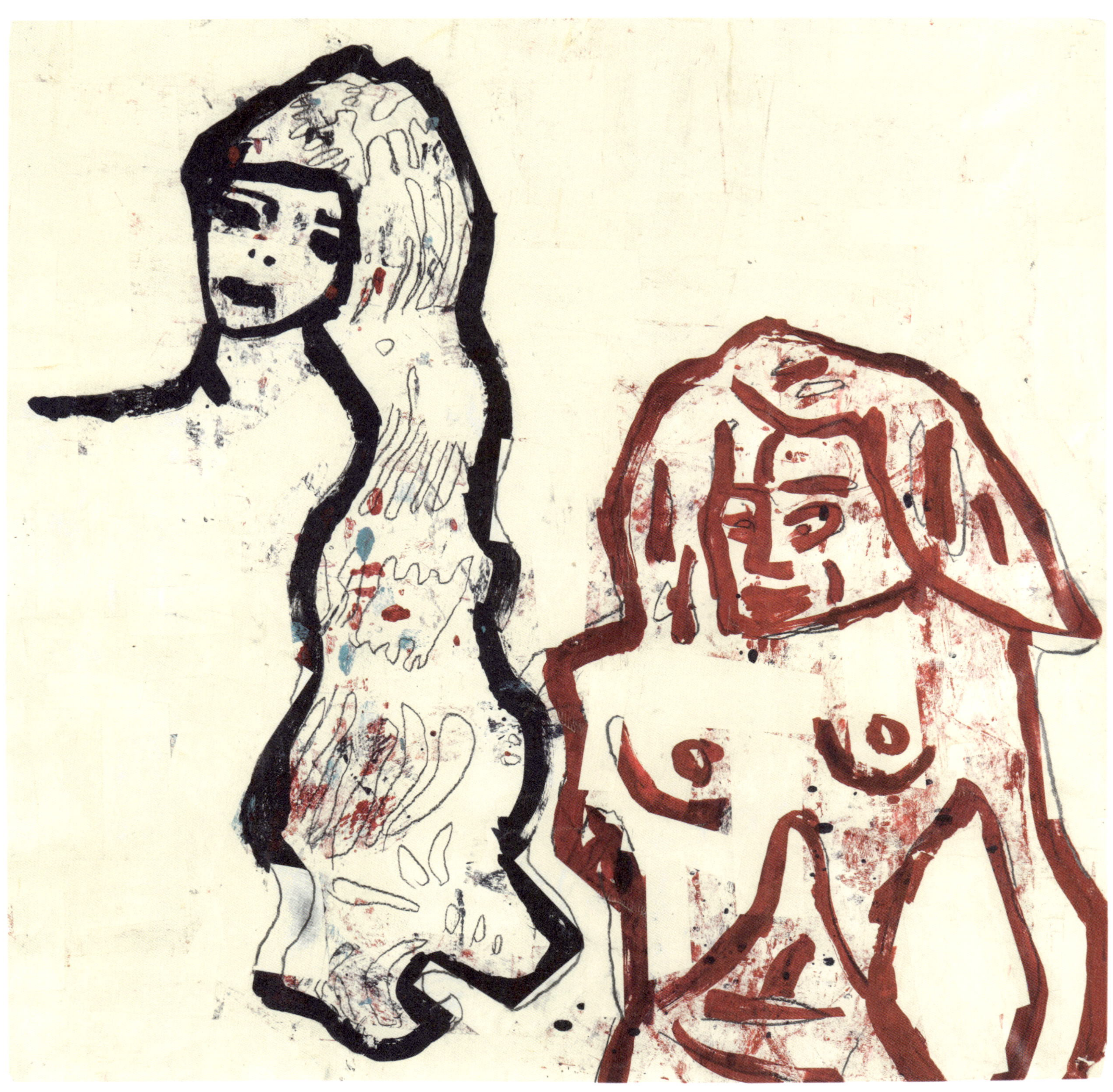

Untitled (Boy + Girl) 1983 acrylic, tempera, graphite and paper collage on paper 36 x 36 in 91.4 x 91.4 cm

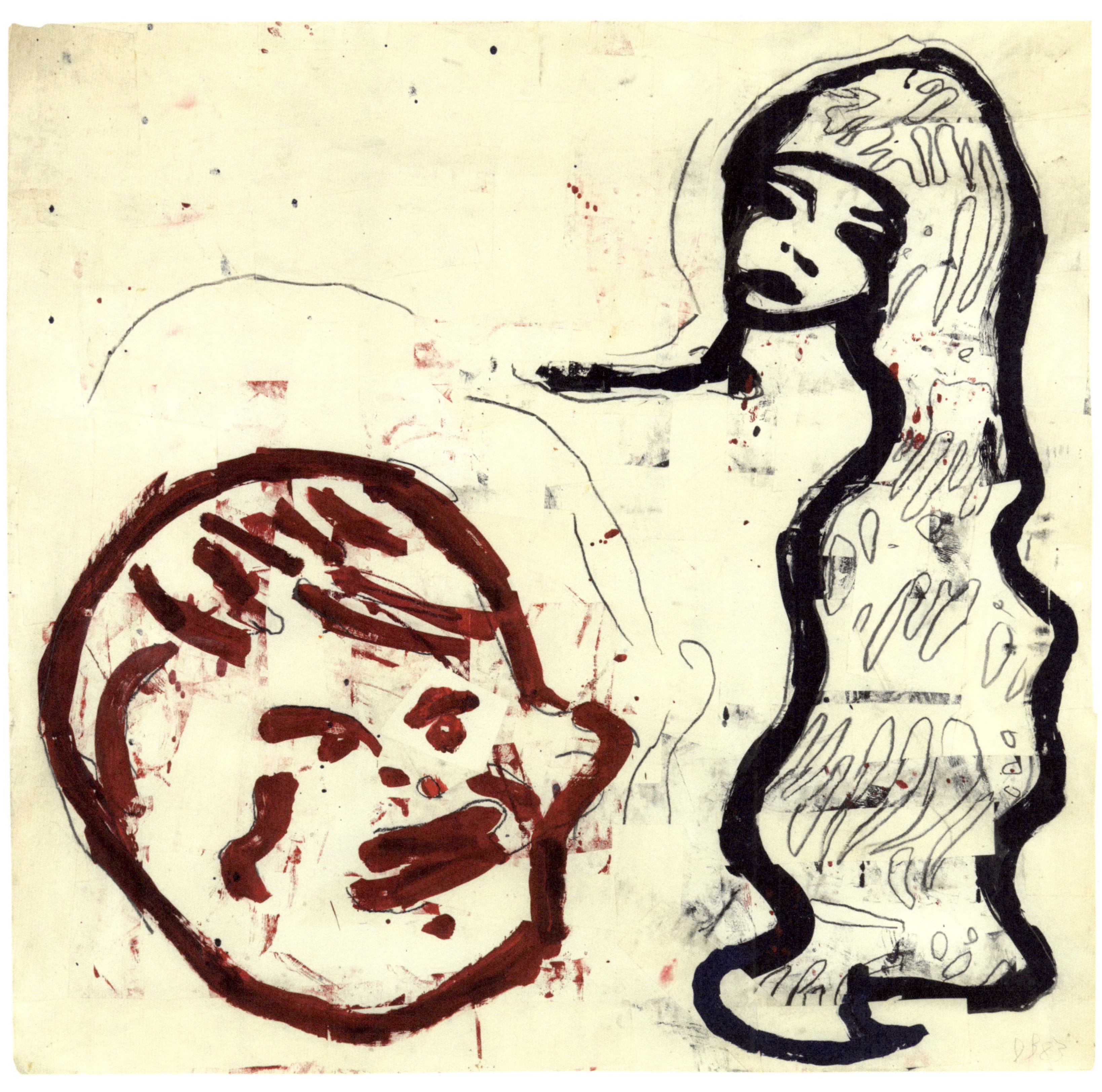

Study for "Sins of Omission" 1983 acrylic and paper collage on paper 36 x 36 in 91.4 x 91.4 cm

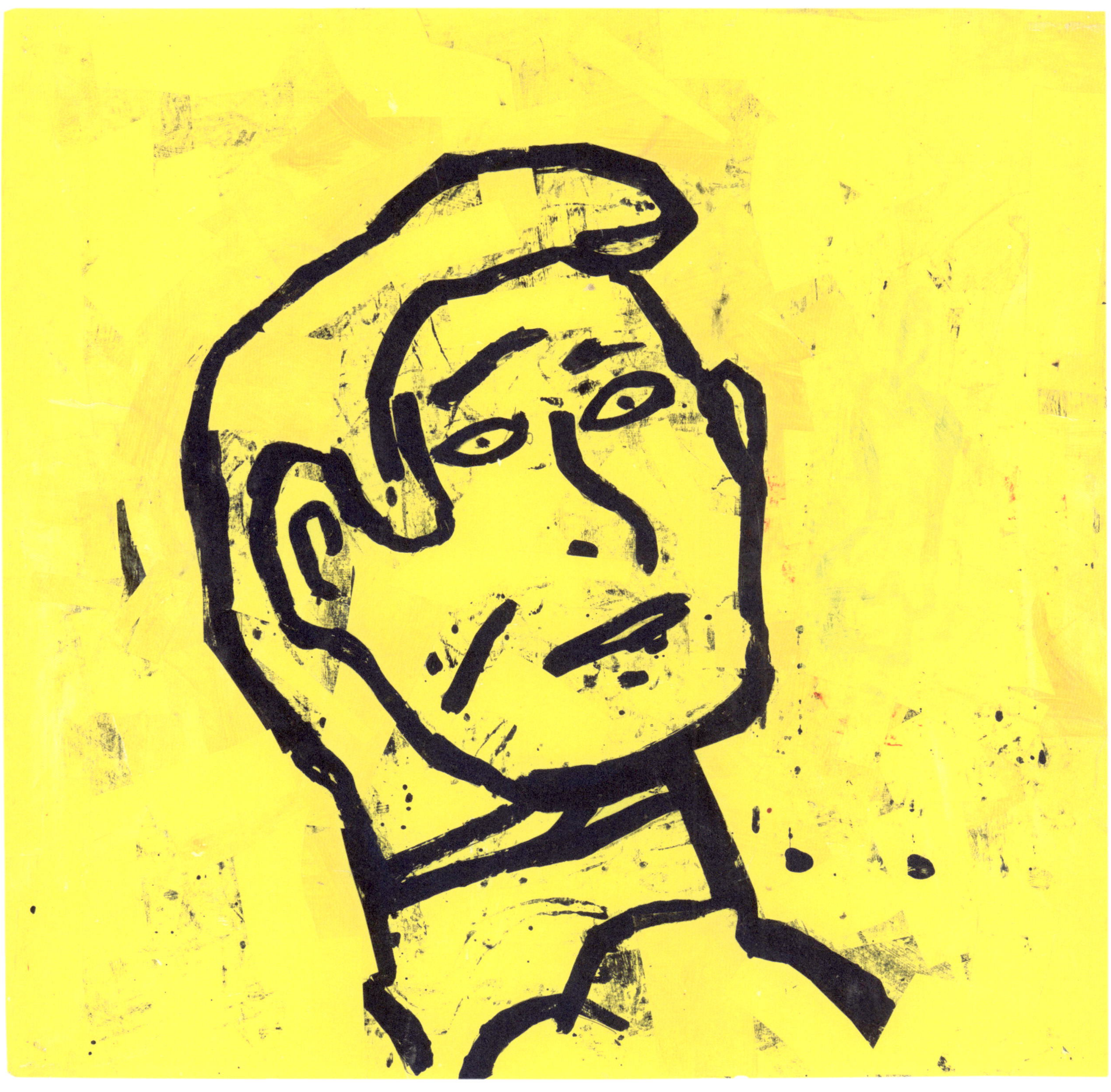

Untitled (Hello) 1983 acrylic and paper collage on paper 36 x 36 in 91.4 x 91.4 cm

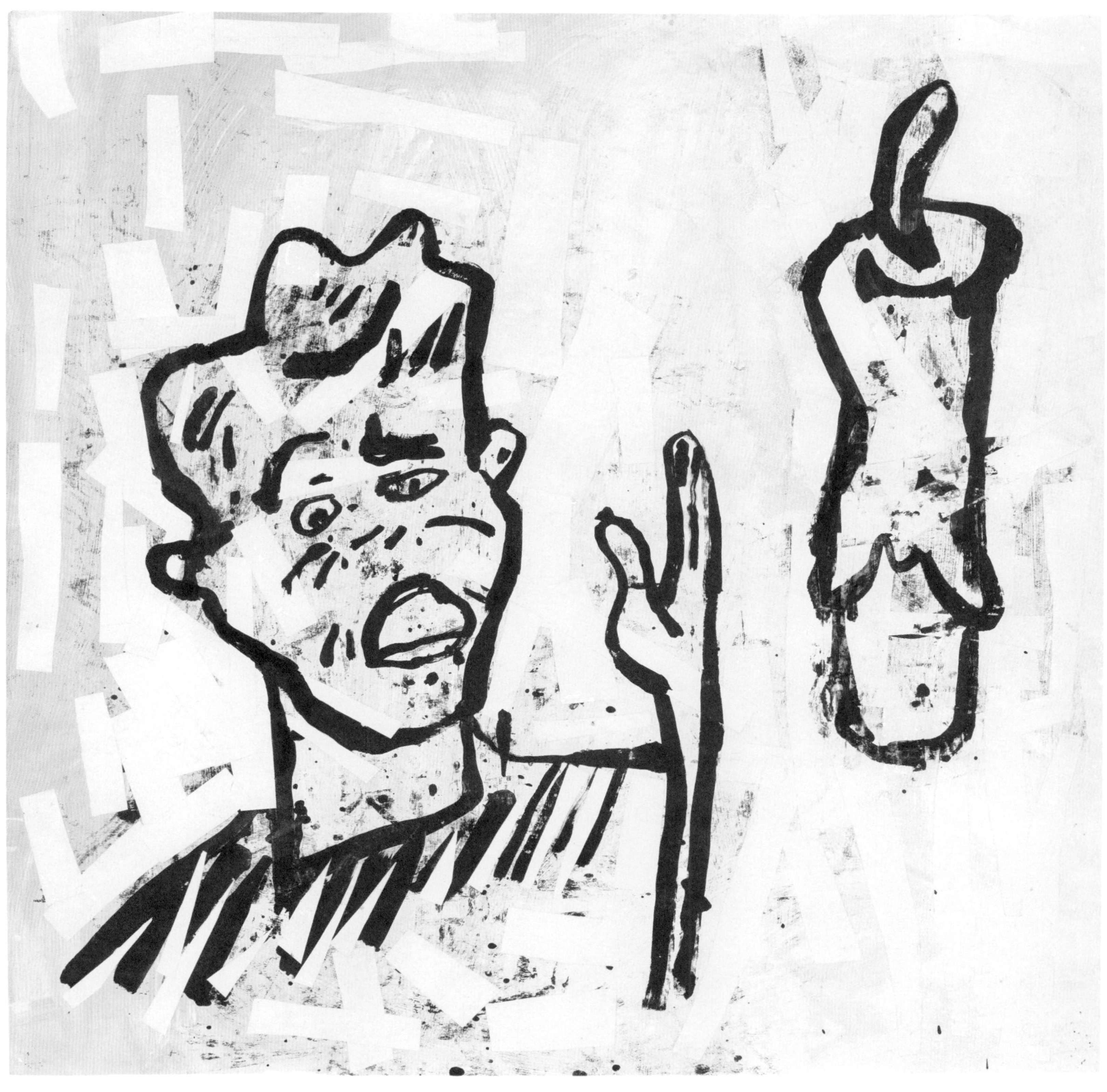

Untitled (2 Boys) 1983 acrylic, tempera, graphite and paper collage on paper 36 x 36 in 91.4 x 91.4 cm

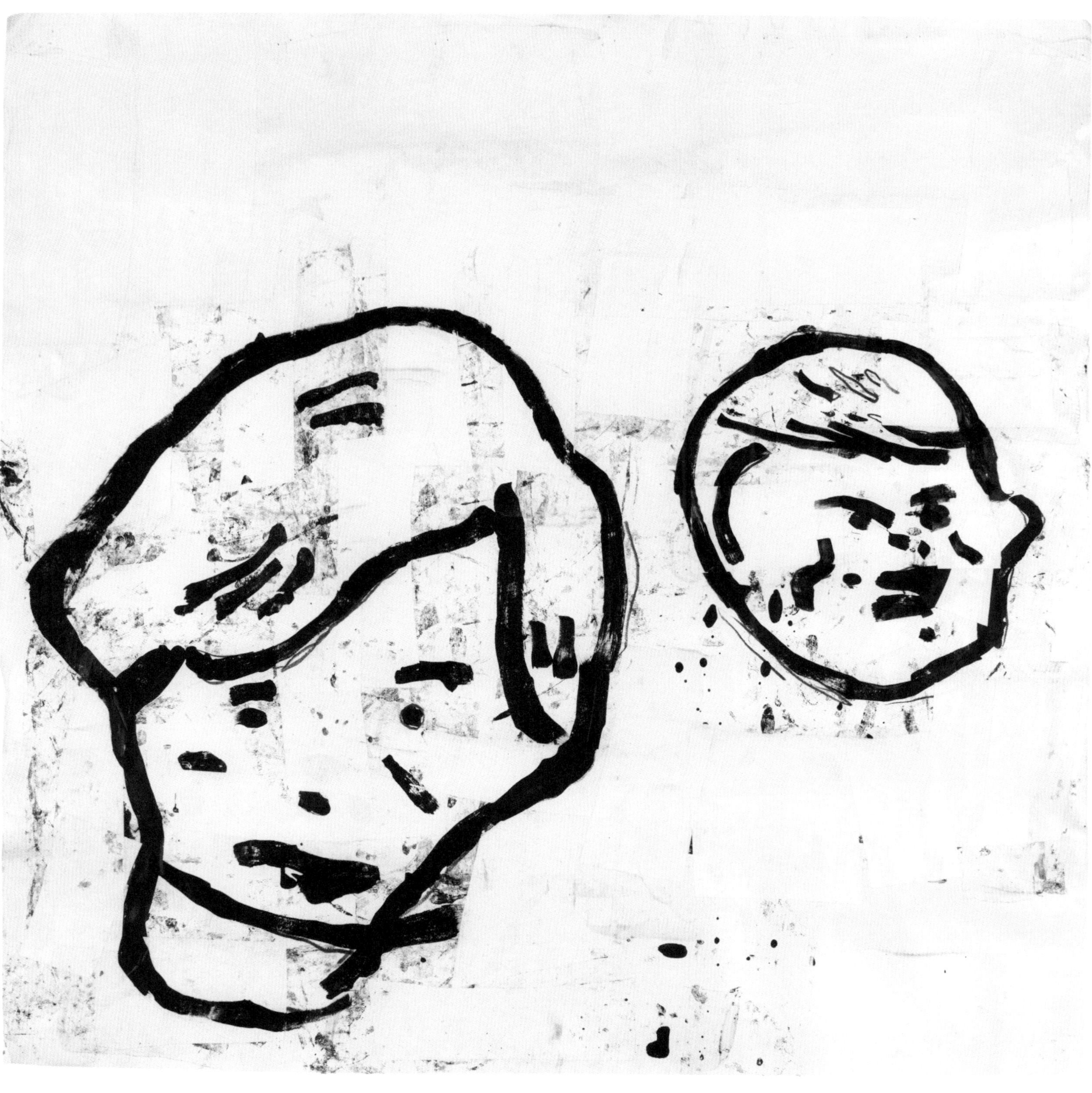

Study for "die Fahne Hoch" 1984 acrylic and paper collage on paper 36 x 36 in 91.4 x 91.4 cm

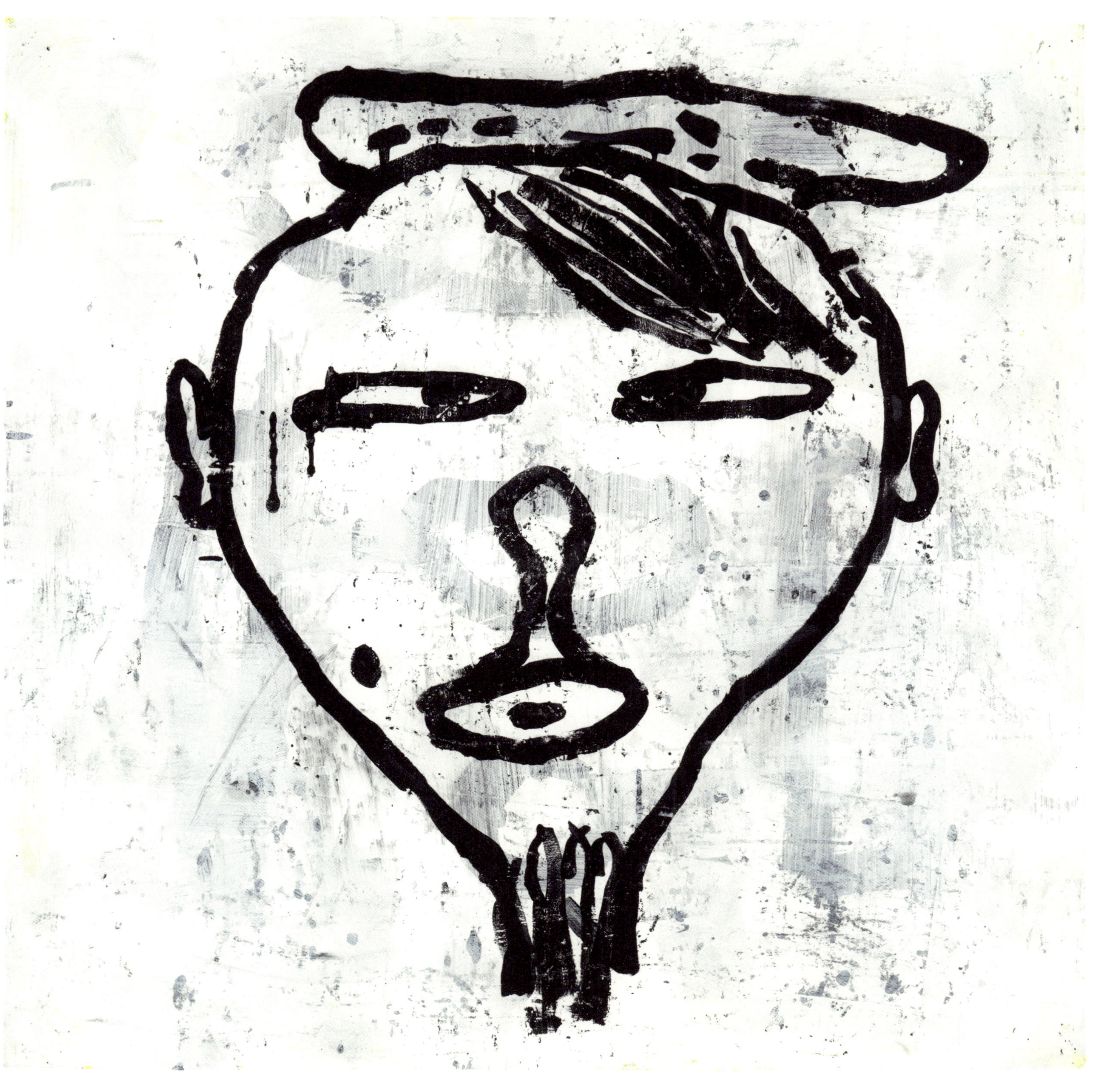

Afrikareise 1984 acrylic and paper collage on paper 36 x 36 in 91.4 x 91.4 cm

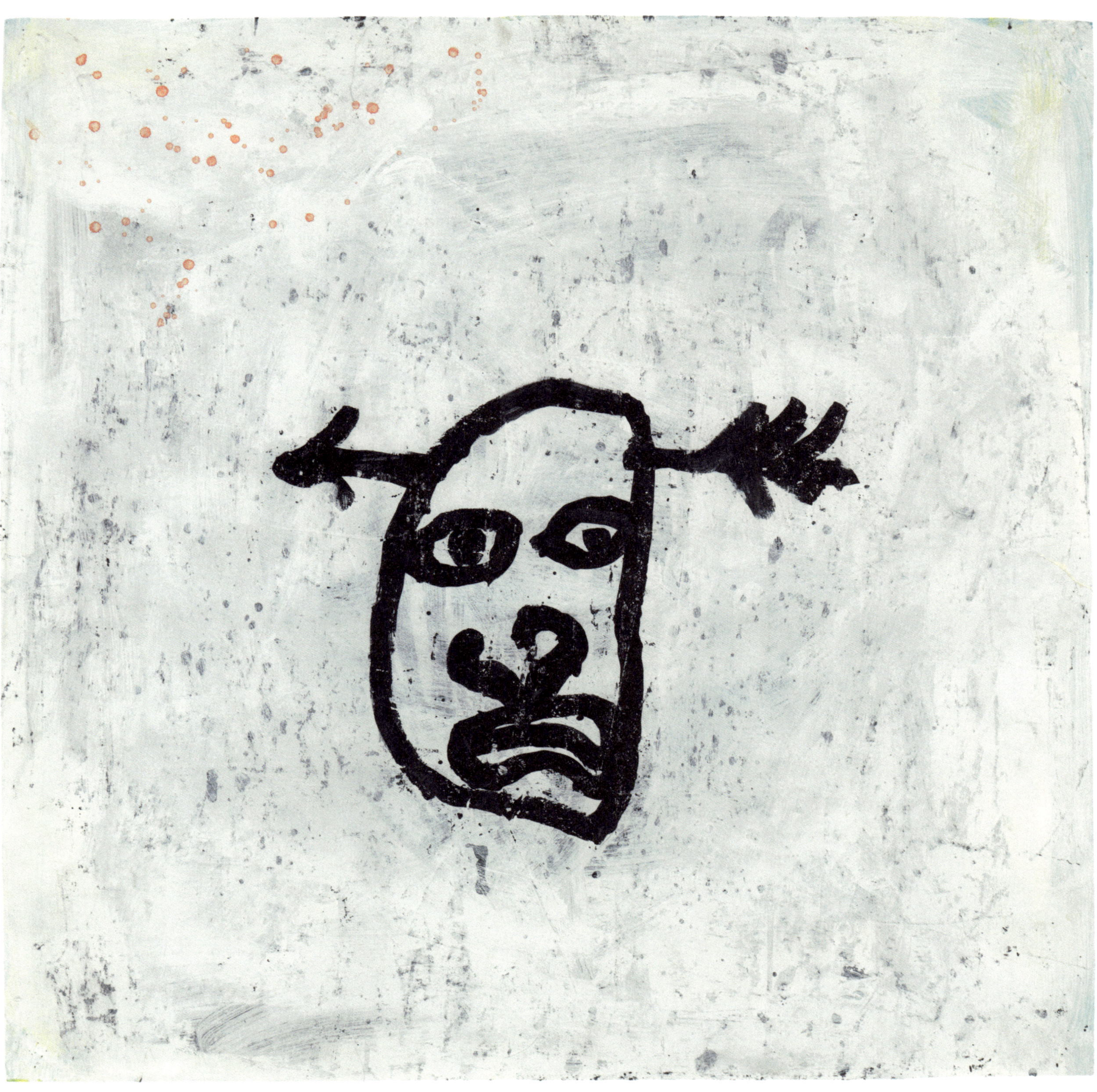

Donald Donald (Study for "Victims of Emigrants") 1984 acrylic and paper collage on paper 36 x 36 in 91.4 x 91.4 cm

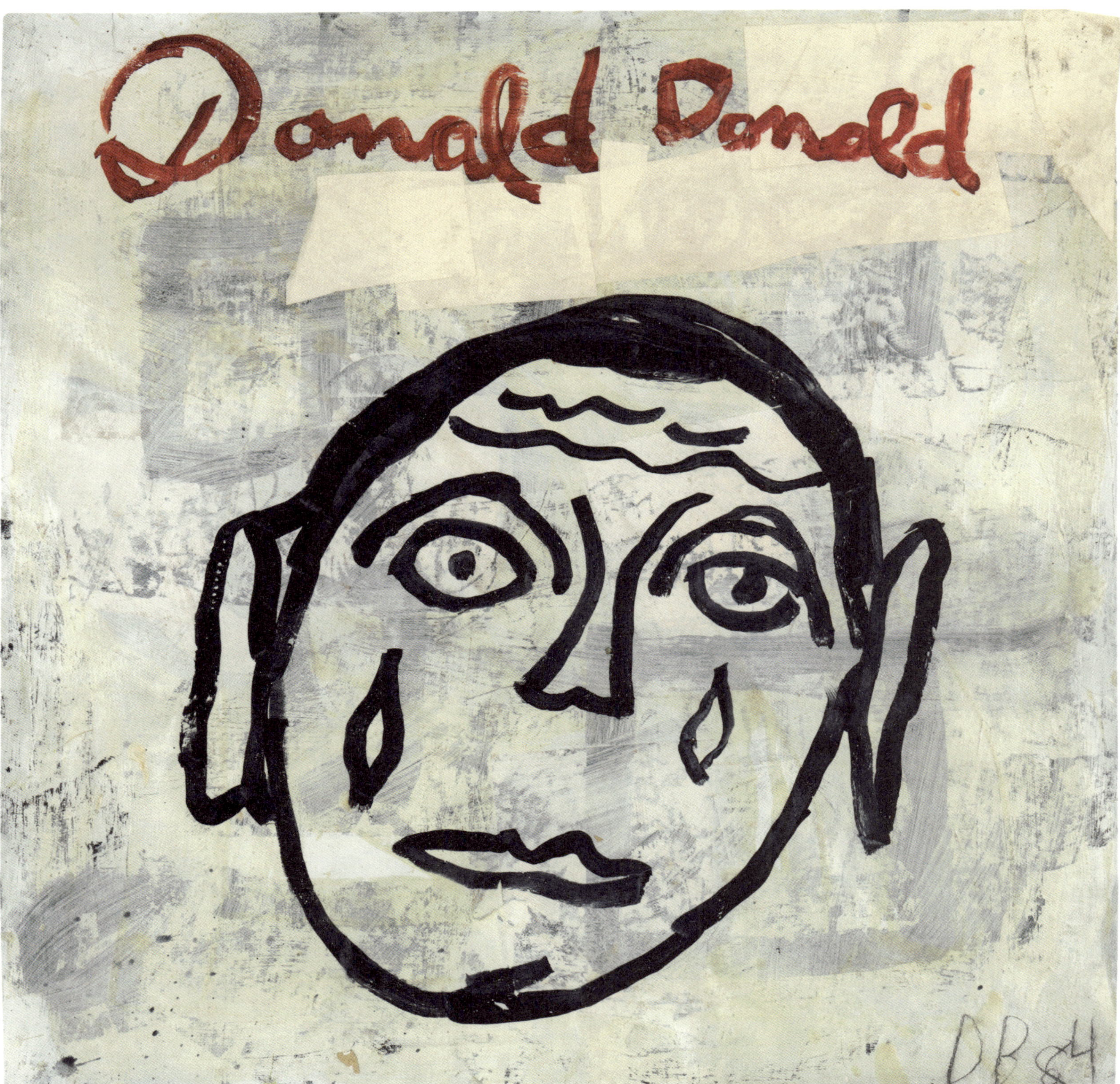

Donald Donald
DB 84

Self Portrait 1984 acrylic and paper collage on paper 36 x 36 in 91.4 x 91.4 cm

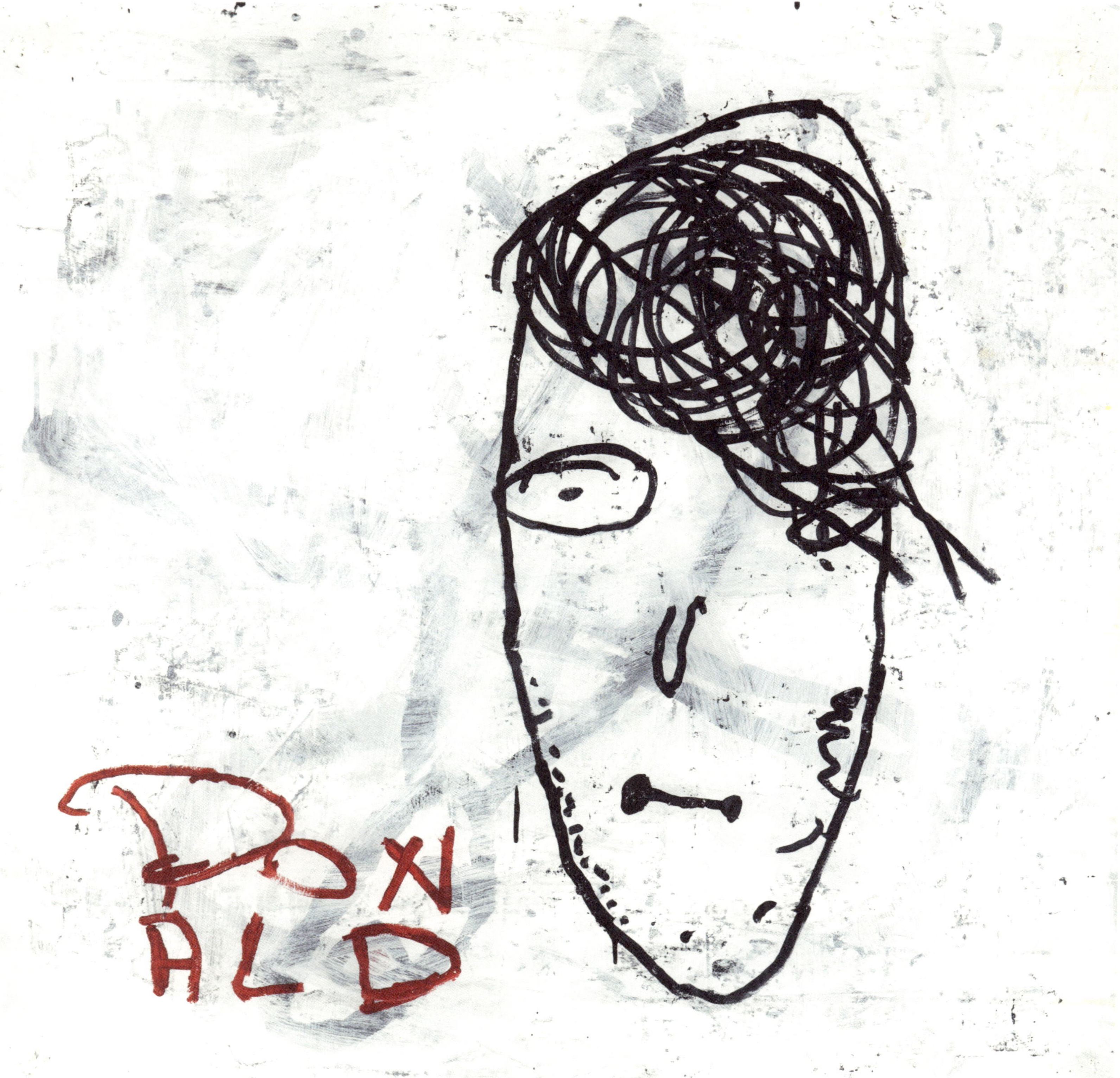

DON
ALD

Head 1984 acrylic and paper collage on paper 36 x 36 in 91.4 x 91.4 cm

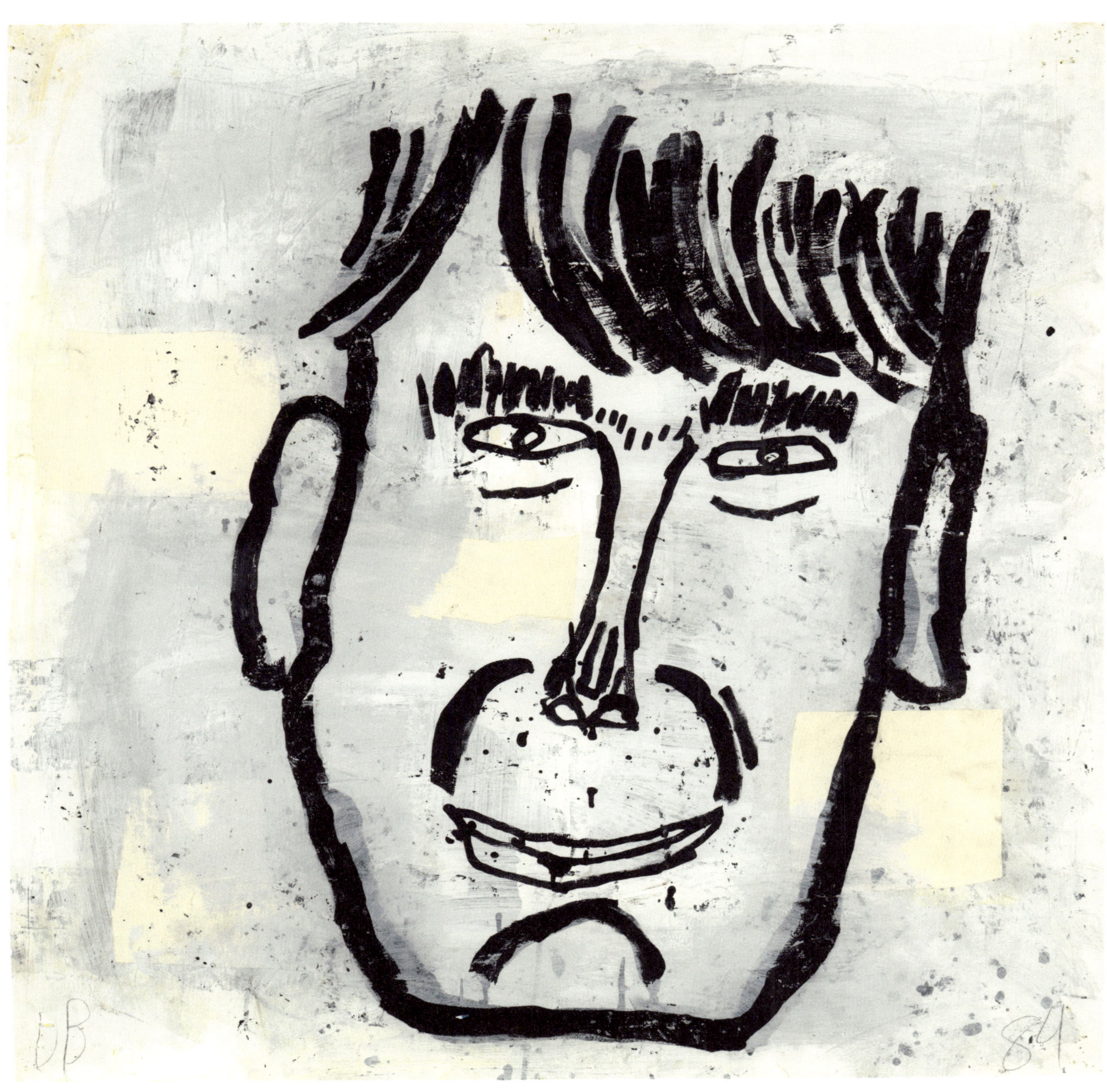
DB
84

Head 1984 acrylic and paper collage on paper 36 x 36 in 91.4 x 91.4 cm

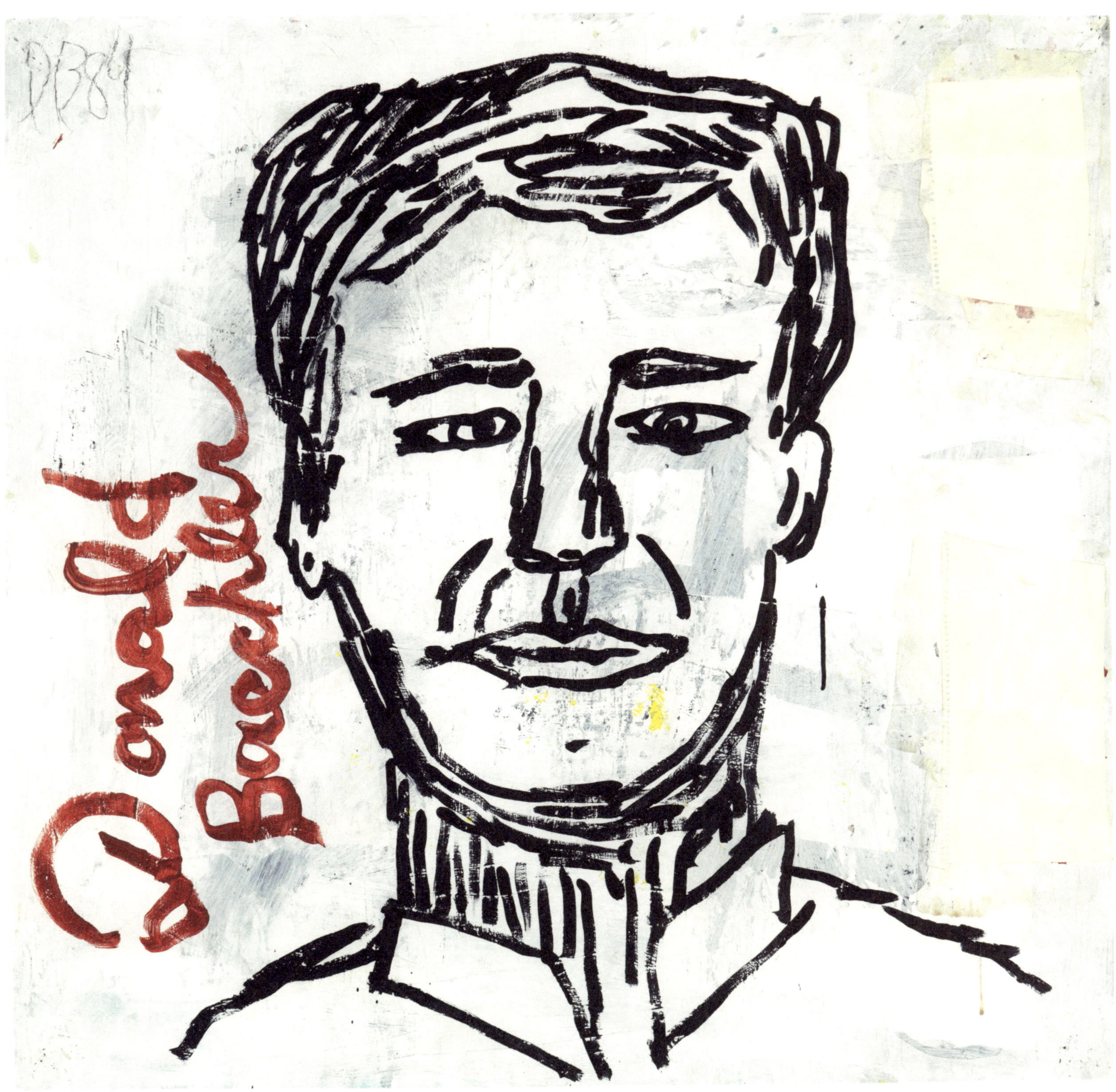

DB84
Donald Baechler

BIOGRAPHY

Born 1956, Hartford, Connecticut

Lives and works in New York

Donald Baechler's creative process begins amidst a vast collection of popular images and objects, the archives of years of photographing, looking and gathering. His paintings are condensed versions of a cumulative process, built in fragments and layers to create what he calls an "illusion of history." The artist cites Cy Twombly and Giotto as primary influences. He has had recent solo exhibitions at the Fisher Landau Center for Art, the Kunsthalle Merano, Italy and the Museum der Moderne, Rupertinum, Salzburg. Baechler's work is in the collections of The Museum of Modern Art, The Whitney Museum of American Art, The Solomon R. Guggenheim Museum, The Museum of Contemporary Art, Los Angeles and The Centre George Pompidou, Musée National d'Art Moderne, Paris among other notable institutions worldwide.

Donald Baechler

EARLY WORK 1980 TO 1984

PUBLISHED ON THE OCCASION OF THE 2015 CHEIM & READ EXHIBITION. DESIGN JOHN CHEIM. ESSAY DAVID RIMANELLI. EDITOR ELLEN ROBINSON. PHOTOGRAPHY BRIAN BUCKLEY. FRONTISPIECE © TIMOTHY GREENFIELD-SANDERS, 1982. PRINTER TRIFOLIO. ISBN 978-1-944316-00-6.